D0984071

The Platform of Time

The Platform of Time
Memoirs of Family and Friends

Virginia Woolf

Edited by S.P. Rosenbaum

WITHDRAWN

ET REMOTISSIMA PROPE

THE PENNSYLVANIA STATE UNIVERSITY
COMMONWEALTH CAMPUS LIBRARIES
BRANDYWINE

Published by Hesperus Press Limited
4 Rickett Street, London sw6 1RU
www.hesperuspress.com

First published by Hesperus Press Limited, 2007

Virginia Woolf texts: Copyright © The Estate of Virginia Woolf 2007
Introduction and other editorial matter: Copyright © S.P. Rosenbaum 2007

'Julia Margaret Cameron', 'An Obituary of Lady Strachey' and 'The
Enchanted Organ' from *The Essays of Virginia Woolf* edited by Andrew
McNeillie: Copyright © 1988, 1994 by Quentin Bell and Angelica Garnett,
reprinted by permission of Harcourt, Inc.

Vanessa Bell's Memoir of Julian Bell: Copyright © 2005, The Estate of Vanessa
Bell, reprinted by kind permission of Angelica and Henrietta Garnett.

Leonard Woolf's obituary of Lady Ritchie: Copyright © 1919, The Estate of
Leonard Woolf, reprinted by permission of the University of Sussex, and the
Society of Authors as their representative.

Letter of Julian Bell to Virginia Woolf reprinted by kind permission of Anne
Olivier Bell.

'Miss Case' from *A Passionate Apprentice* by Virginia Woolf, edited by
Mitchell A. Leaska, published by Hogarth Press: Copyright © 1990, Quentin
Bell and Angelica Garnett, reprinted by permission of The Random House
Group Ltd.

The Estate of Virginia Woolf asserts the moral right of Virginia Woolf to be
identified as the author of the Memoirs.

S.P. Rosenbaum asserts his moral right to be identified as the author of the
transcription, editorial apparatus and introduction.

Designed and typeset by Fraser Muggeridge studio
Printed in Jordan by the Jordan National Press

ISBN: 1-84391-709-2
ISBN13: 978-1-84391-709-0

All rights reserved. This book is sold subject to the condition that it shall not be
resold, lent, hired out or otherwise circulated without the express prior consent
of the publisher.

Contents

Introduction

On 25th April 1940, Virginia Woolf wrote in her diary, 'I was thinking of my memoirs. The platform of time. How I see father from the 2 angles. As a child condemning; as a woman of 58 understanding – I shd say tolerating. Both views true?' The memoirs Woolf was referring to were the notes that became the great autobiographical fragment she called 'Sketch of the Past'. When writing these notes a year earlier, she thought she had possibly discovered a form for them:

> That is, to make them include the present – at least enough of the present to serve as platform to stand upon. It would be interesting to make the two people, I now, I then, come out in contrast. And further, this past is much affected by the present moment. What I write today I should not write in a year's time. ('Sketch of the Past', 2nd May 1939)

The intersection of the present and the past viewed from the platform of time informs not only 'Sketch of the Past' but all her memoir writings.

These memoirs have yet to be systematically collected and edited. Virginia Woolf's two longest memoirs, for example, are usually mistitled. When they were published along with three Memoir Club Papers in *Moments of Being* (1976, expanded 1985, re-edited 2002), the first was called 'Reminiscences', but Woolf is not reminiscencing; she is writing an untitled biography of her sister Vanessa Bell in the form of an autobiographical letter addressed to Vanessa's infant son Julian. And 'Sketch of the Past' she called just that – without articles, definite or indefinite. More important is the omission from *Moments of Being* of a third extended memoir that Virginia Woolf wrote for herself after Julian Bell was killed. Julian's brother Quentin included less than half of this memoir as an appendix to his aunt's biography. With the complete text that is given here, however, one can see the extent to which it is a family memoir illuminating those that were published in *Moments of Being*. A briefer, unpublished memoir by Vanessa Bell written shortly after she learned of her son's death is a moving addition to Virginia's remembrance of Julian.

In addition to her memoir of Julian Bell, Virginia Woolf wrote a number of other briefer memoirs of family and friends that are now brought together in *The Platform of Time*. These include the two short recollections of her father that she wrote more than a quarter of a century apart. Next are accounts of three remarkable aunts, and then memoirs of four friends: Lady Strachey, the mother of Lytton; Roger Fry, whose biography she would write; her teacher and friend Janet Case; and the flamboyant, aristocratic Ottoline Morrell. The memoir of Case (an anonymous obituary letter to *The Times* reprinted here for the first time) is supplemented by a sketch that was written when Virginia was her pupil and which provides another 'I now, I then' concurrence. Two memoirs of occasions follow those of her friends. The first resulted from a request of the Woolfs' friend Margaret Llewelyn Davies for an introduction to a book of memoirs by working women. Protesting that books should stand on their own feet, and she would rather be drowned than write a foreword to one, Virginia used her and Leonard's memories of a Women's Co-operative Guild congress and visits to the Guild's headquarters to write two introductory versions. The revised one reprinted here separately for the first time is the foreword she actually wrote for the book. The second occasional memoir survives only as a fragment of notes for a talk that Virginia Woolf gave towards the end of her life on the celebrated *Dreadnought* Hoax of 1910, in which she participated. The notes are augmented by an interview Virginia gave at the time – indeed, apparently the only interview that she ever gave. *The Platform of Time* concludes with three post-*Orlando* memoir fantasies, not written for publication, which were based on the Stephen family cook and on Woolf's Bloomsbury friends, the obscure Saxon Sydney-Turner and the world-famous John Maynard Keynes.

When brought together, the briefer memoirs and the longer one of Julian Bell display various interconnections. There are the relationships of Julian Bell and Roger Fry, of Virginia Woolf's three aunts with one another and with Leslie Stephen, who also knew Lady Strachey. Janet Case and Margaret Llewelyn Davies are connected in several ways in Woolf's memories, as are Janet Case and Julian Bell. And the family cook is associated by Virginia with working women of the Co-operative Guild. Interrelated themes appear as well among Virginia Woolf's briefer memoirs: class awareness, education and the status of women, Cambridge college life and values, understanding visual and literary art, war and the military patriarchy, and finally the platform of time itself and how the present conditions one's views of the past and the writing of memoirs. Though a number of the memoirs are obituaries of one kind or another, their tone is never mortuary and can be humorous, ironic, even satiric.

The introductions to Virginia Woolf's memoirs of family and friends describe the subjects of Woolf's memoir writings and the circumstances – the platforms – of their composition. Identifications of people, places and groups alluded to in the memoirs are given at the end, followed by editorial notes listing the sources of the memoirs and explaining editorial procedures, and then by acknowledgements and a list of works cited or consulted.

– S.P. Rosenbaum, 2007

The Platform of Time
Memoirs of Family and Friends

I
Julian Bell

Virginia Woolf learned of the death of her nephew Julian Bell on 20th July 1937. He had died of his wounds while serving as an ambulance driver in the Spanish Civil War. Virginia cared for her grief-stricken sister in London until the 29th, then Virginia and Leonard Woolf drove Vanessa to Charleston, her Sussex home. The next day Virginia began an unfinished memoir of Julian. And sometime between the 20th and the end of the month Vanessa too made brief memoir notes about her son.

Virginia Woolf's and Vanessa Bell's memoirs of Julian Bell illuminate each other as autobiographical as well as literary writings. Although Vanessa makes no mention of Virginia in her memoir, its fragmentary pictures display the relationship with her son that so intrigued her sister. Virginia's much longer text centres on the deep love for Vanessa that both Virginia and Julian felt as a bond between themselves. Behind the memoir impulse of mother and aunt was a tradition of ancestral recollection, the most recent being their father Leslie Stephen's memoirs, written for his children after the death of their mother, which they dubbed *The Mausoleum Book*. Virginia and Vanessa were not writing for their families, however, and neither attempted to express anything like the Victorian lamentations that had echoed through their adolescence. Indeed there is a notable lack of sentimentality in these two intensely felt memoirs, for also in the background of their writing was The Memoir Club. Virginia and Vanessa had been meeting with the friends and relatives known now as the Bloomsbury Group since 1920 to read one another their intimate, sometimes ironic short memoirs. Yet Virginia's and Vanessa's memoirs were not written for or ever presented to the Club. Nor was Virginia's written for Vanessa, as has sometimes been said; there is no indication either sister saw the other's memoir. Theirs were private rather than family or social memoirs, written to relieve the immediacy of their grief and, as Virginia says at the start of hers, to fix their memories before the passage of time made them unreal. Both were left incomplete, like Julian's own brief life.

More than half of Virginia Woolf's memoir and all of Vanessa Bell's remained unpublished until 2005. They appear here in book form for the first time. Virginia Woolf's memoir is supplemented here first with her earlier satirical sketch of Julian and with excerpts from the letters she mentions in her memoir (one of which was thought lost when her letters were edited), along with part of Julian's reply.

When Julian Bell's brother Quentin included excerpts from his aunt's memoir as an appendix to his biography of Virginia Woolf (written more than a generation ago now), he did so 'in the belief that it illuminates Virginia's own character and personality'. That it certainly does. But in omitting 'some less relevant passages', Quentin altered the tentative narrative shape of a memoir Virginia felt she had not yet developed properly. First of all, Quentin removed most of the references to himself. He then deleted Virginia's recurring comparison of Julian with her beloved brother (Julian) Thoby Stephen, who died young thirty years before, and for whom Julian Bell was named. Also cut was Virginia's emphasis on how Julian Bell had changed after his return from teaching English in China. Some disparaging references to the poets Stephen Spender, W.H. Auden and John Lehmann were removed, along with Virginia's reference to Julian's 'failure' at Cambridge (his two fellowship dissertations were unsuccessful) and her speculation on his standing with those of his generation such as Spender, Auden, or Lehmann, with whom he had published poems in *New Signatures*, the Woolfs' Hogarth Press anthology of 1932. Allusions to Bloomsbury friends such as Roger Fry, E.M. Forster and Desmond MacCarthy were left out, along with Julian's criticism of Bloomsbury's attitudes toward education. All mention of Julian's love affairs was also dropped, including the scene in which Virginia and Julian quarrel over her sending his Chinese girlfriend away. (The girlfriend in question may have been Su Hua Ling Chen – to use the name she gave in her memoirs – the wife of Julian's Dean at Wuhan University; it was the discovery of their affair that led to Julian's resignation.)

In addition to changing the form of her memoir, Quentin Bell's deletions also minimise the degree to which Virginia Woolf's is a family memoir. Though written for herself to make Julian's death real and to preserve his personal presence, Woolf's memoir is inevitably about her family. Julian's death recalls Thoby's, which leads Virginia to muse on Julian's Stephen and Bell heredity. Love of Vanessa is described as 'the deepest union' between Virginia herself and Julian, but it is a union that complicates their relationship. 'What an uncomfortable relation, Aunt & nephew', she exclaimed in her diary before Julian went to China (21st February 1935). Earlier she had acknowledged him in the playful preface to *Orlando* for his 'singularly penetrating, if severe, criticism', as opposed to Quentin, who was 'an old and valued collaborator'. Virginia's and Julian's was a deeply affectionate yet wary relationship, and even finally a resentful one because of the pain Julian caused Vanessa by his decision to go to Spain. Julian's father Clive and his uncle Leonard Woolf appear and reappear in the memoir, as does Quentin himself. And there are references to Angelica Bell, Quentin's half-sister, and to her father, Vanessa's long-time companion Duncan Grant.

Then there is 'the damned literary question' of Virginia's attitude toward Julian's writing that she reverts to in her memoir, and which becomes unavoidably a family question as well. Virginia was glad the Hogarth Press had published Julian's second volume of poetry, *Work for the Winter*, in 1936, but Virginia was never enthusiastic about his poetry. 'The damned literary question' comes into the unpublished dramatic skit 'JB' included here, which Virginia wrote around 1931 to mock affectionately her nephew's attempts to write poetry. Sometime later, probably after Julian's death, she wrote on the manuscript of the skit, 'This was a malicious but very amusing satire upon Julian Bell.' The sketch may have been intended for the family newspaper, the *Charleston Bulletin*, in response to Julian and Quentin's earlier satires of Virginia there. Virginia herself and Vanessa appear in the satire along with Grace Higgens, the cook at Charleston, and John Lehmann, whose poems the Hogarth Press published in 1931. There are allusions to Julian's King's College tutor F.L. Lucas, to the philosopher Richard Braithwaite, and to the dissertations Julian wrote on Pope's poetry and on the ethics of G.E. Moore (whose famous epigraph to *Principia Ethica* – Bishop Butler's 'Everything is what it is, and not another thing' – is made fun of).

Julian's essay-letter on Roger Fry, which Leonard and Virginia turned down for their press, was a further literary difficulty. Julian appears to have written two letters about Roger Fry for Virginia that are sometimes confused. The first letter, now lost (from which Woolf quotes in her biography of Fry), was in response to her asking Julian for biographical anecdotes about Fry. It was Julian's second essay-letter that Virginia regretfully criticised and that the Hogarth Press declined but eventually published posthumously.

Also a family matter is the issue of Spain. Spain raised questions for Virginia Woolf such as why Julian, now matured from teaching in China, felt he had to go to the war – questions of what others of his generation were doing, and of how his decision tormented Vanessa even after he was persuaded to serve with Spanish Medical Aid rather than fight with the International Brigade. The Spanish Civil War became a literary question too, for Julian's death interrupted Virginia's writing of her polemical book *Three Guineas*. Relevant to that book is her conviction that strong feelings, which can be both fine and wrong, must be controlled by reason.

From the problem of Spain Woolf's memoir breaks off to return to views of Julian as a boy, a student, an Apostle, a lover, before the continuing presence of Quentin Bell ends the memoir and returns it to the present.

The platform from which Virginia Woolf looks at Julian's brief life is necessarily lower than any of Woolf's other memoirs. 'I am so composed,' she wrote at its opening, 'that nothing is real unless I write it.' Time, she continued, 'does not destroy people… but it brushes away the actual personal presence.' There is a sense of urgency in her effort to preserve in words, to realise through them – in the literal sense of making real – Julian's presence as it fades in memory. Her memoir is in itself an affecting modernist expression of mourning and loss without consolation for a war-dead nephew.

When read in its entirety, however, Woolf's memoir of Julian takes on added significance in relation to her two other substantial memoirs: the early autobiographical letter on Vanessa, and the late work of autobiographical art 'Sketch of the Past'. These works constitute Virginia Woolf's most substantial memoirs, and taken together in their unabridged form, they extend one another. To see this it is worth glancing at some of the connections that illuminate Woolf's three unfinished autobiographical works.

In a way Virginia's memoir of Julian, so concerned as it is with the relations of son and mother, nephew and aunt, sister and sister, has its beginning in the life of Vanessa that Virginia began to write for Julian before he was born. (This memoir, mistitled 'Reminiscences', is published along with 'Sketch of the Past' and her Memoir Club papers in *Moments of Being*.) By writing his mother's life for her nephew, Virginia continued in her ironic way the family-memoir tradition of her father's *Mausoleum Book*. Vanessa is identified as 'your mother', Julia and Leslie Stephen as 'your grandmother', 'your grandfather', and so on. The havoc that the deaths of Julia Stephen and then her daughter Stella Duckworth wrought in the family, especially for Vanessa and Virginia, is essentially the story being told to the infant Julian. Virginia's narrative ends when Vanessa's biography becomes inseparable from Virginia's autobiography – when, as the narrator informs her baby nephew, 'we' must now stand for his mother and herself.

'Sketch of the Past' is a memoir and a meditation on memoir-writing. It starts again with Vanessa, who urges her sister to begin her memoirs before it is too late. This provides Virginia with a departure point and a way of relieving with autobiography the labour of writing Roger Fry's biography. Julian Bell does not figure in the 'Sketch of the Past', which stops at the end of the nineteenth century. But directly relevant to Virginia's memoir of Julian is the account of her memoir-habit. She describes how her 'shock-receiving capacity' makes her a writer because she feels the shock is

> ... a revelation of some order; it is a token of some real thing behind appearances; and I make it real by putting it into words. It is only by putting it into words that I make it whole; this wholeness means that it has lost its power to hurt me; it gives me, perhaps because by doing so I take away the pain, a great delight to put the severed parts together.

From this she goes on to express her conviction that behind what she thinks of as the cotton wool of everyday appearance is a reality of moments of ecstatic being. In these moments the world and its inhabitants are connected in a pattern, as parts of a work of art ('Sketch of the Past', 18th April 1939).

If looked at as a kind of commentary on her memoir of Julian Bell, Virginia's description in 'Sketch of the Past' further explains her need to write about him – her need to come to literary terms with the shock and pain of his death, to preserve the memory of his reality, to try and understand it as part of a meaningful whole. But for several reasons she is not really able to do this in her memoir of Julian. First of all it was the unnatural violence of his death that she says later in her diary she could not make fit anywhere (12th October 1937). Here was no indifferent vanquishing process of mortality, as with Roger Fry's death or Thoby Stephen's or her mother's, against whom she could fight with her brain and heart (19th September 1934). Then there was the question of Spain, again, and what it meant to Julian and his generation. Without an answer to this she cannot in her memoir make his death part of the patterned reality in a work of art. Finally, there was the nature of her own grief for Julian. In 'Sketch of the Past' Virginia, writing of her mother's death, remembered wanting to laugh at a nurse's sobbing and saying to herself 'as I have often done at moments of crisis since, "I feel nothing whatever"' ('Sketch of the Past', 28th May 1939). At Roger Fry's funeral nearly forty years later she recalled in her diary that scene and experienced the same lack of emotion, which she put down to the writer's analytic temperament (as described by Maupassant):

> I remember turning aside at mother's bed, when she had died, & Stella took us in, to laugh, secretly, at the nurse crying. She's pretending, I said: aged 13. & was afraid I was not feeling enough. So now. (12th September 1934)

With Julian's death it was different. Now there was no detachment from grief. She could write about his life in her memoir, but not about his death in her diary. After the terrible news,

Virginia made no entries for nearly three weeks. It was during this time that she wrote her memoir. Resuming the diary on 6th August, she then noted,

> Its odd that I can hardly bring myself, with all my verbosity – the expression mania which is inborn in me – to say anything about Julian's death – I mean about that last 10 days in London. But one must get into the current again. That was a complete break; almost a blank; like a blow on the head: a shrivelling up. Going around to 8 [Fitzroy Street, Vanessa's studio] that night; & then all the other times, & sitting there. When Roger died I noticed: & blamed myself; yet it was a great relief I think. Here there was no relief. An incredible suffering – to watch it – an accident, & someone bleeding. Then I thought the death of a child is childbirth again; sitting there listening. (6th August 1937)

The watching and listening was what Vanessa now needed. As she wrote to Vita Sackville West a little later, 'I cannot ever say how Virginia has helped me,' and hoped some day Vita could tell her (16th August 1937).

In 'Sketch of the Past' Virginia notes that representative 'scene-making' is the way she sums up the past, making a knot of its innumerable threads, and she speculates that her capacity for scene-making may be the origin of her literary impulse. How she experiences scenes is mystically described again as moments of being in which she is ecstatically flooded with reality ('Sketch of the Past', 11th October 1940). Virginia Woolf's memoir of Julian can also be seen as a series of scenes, beginning with his return from China and continuing with scenes of childhood. But there are no revelatory moments of reality in them. Appearance and reality do not figure here as they will in 'Sketch of the Past'. Another reason for the absence of patterned moments of reality may have been Vanessa's connection with the memoir. While discussing her scene-making capacity in 'Sketch of the Past' Virginia remarks that her relation to Vanessa – notably described as 'a close conspiracy' – was one that lay too deep for scenes (15th November 1940). In Virginia's memoir of Julian, Vanessa does not appear prominently in any of the scenes.

The writing that Woolf's memoir of Julian Bell most plainly connects with, however, is the work she was doing when he was killed. She had just finished the obituary letter-memoir for *The Times* on Janet Case, her Greek teacher and friend (which is reprinted here, in section three). Virginia signed the letter as by an old pupil, in accordance with the involved need for literary anonymity that Virginia in her memoir of Julian will compare with his too personal writings. The contrast of Julian's life with the unassuming Janet Case's is manifested in the obituary page of *The Times* for 22nd July, which also included the report of Julian Bell's death.

The memoir of Case was itself a break from the writing of *Three Guineas*, the work with which Julian Bell's death is most often connected. Originally conceived as part of an essay-novel, *Three Guineas* was removed from *The Years* as Virginia separated out the fiction and non-fiction. The miseries of writing *The Years* and the novel's very favourable reception are both mentioned in the memoir of Julian, as are the main themes of *Three Guineas*. Virginia's complex polemic begins with the question of how women can prevent war. In seeking answers *Three Guineas* then proceeds to criticise in its three parts the patriarchal domination of both education and the professions, and then the male psychology of war.

The impact of Julian's death on *Three Guineas* appears in various comments Virginia made in letters and diaries. To Vanessa she wrote she was always wanting to argue posthumously with Julian in the book, 'in fact I wrote it as an argument with him'

(17th August 1937), and in her diaries she noted that *Three Guineas* had supported her like a spine after the horror of his death, and how she was always thinking of Julian when she wrote it (12th March, 3rd June, 1938). Yet it seems an over-simplification to argue, as Julian's brother has in his biography of Virginia Woolf, that *Three Guineas* was to a considerable extent a kind of argument with what Virginia took to be Julian's point of view. The feminist arguments and attitudes expressed in that book, it has been pointed out, were present in her writing long before Julian went to Spain.

The first part of *Three Guineas* dealing with 'educated men's daughters' was drafted before Julian returned from China. Virginia was drafting the second part, dealing with the difficulties of professions for women, when Julian was killed. The third part of *Three Guineas* would be about arms and the man, and it is Julian's attitude to war, his need to go to Spain, that becomes the troubling question of Julian's memoir. It was after reading Julian's posthumously published letter on war and peace to E.M. Forster that Virginia told Vanessa she now understood his point of view (8th September 1937). In the letter to Forster Julian – who was never a communist – argued that to preserve liberal civilisation it was now necessary to give up pacifism and cultivate the military virtues.

In the memoir of Julian, in *Three Guineas*, and in other work, Virginia is quite clear about her own reaction to war, which was to fight it intellectually by writing rather than engage in meaningless, unreal force. Julian, she thought, should have found some other way of supporting the cause of liberty. In his appendix to her biography, Quentin Bell ended the published part of Virginia's memoir at this point. He thus omitted his aunt's expressed conviction that 'one must control feeling with reason' and that Quentin's staying in England to fight politically seemed for her 'harder & finer; more considered; & also as I think a more effective measure...'. Those who talked of Julian's death giving encouragement to the cause she considered emotionally excited by death and glory, though she conceded in a later letter that Spain was a better place to die than Flanders (2nd December 1939).

Quentin Bell's involvement in his brother's memoir, both as a presence and then as a self-effacing editor – which is another form of collaboration with his aunt – displays again the limitations of his abridged version as well as the inevitable family context of the memoir. Just as Virginia Woolf found herself arguing with Julian after his death about war, so Quentin continued to argue posthumously with Virginia over her feminist politics – claiming in another appendix to his own memoirs, for example, that her main contention in *Three Guineas* was the satisfaction that men found in fighting but which women did not. It may be difficult to sort out the family feelings here, with Virginia unhappy about the anguish Julian had caused Vanessa, and Quentin dismayed at Virginia's feminist view of his brother's sacrifice. It seems time, however, to make the complete memoir of Julian Bell available to Virginia Woolf's common readers.

In the *Times* obituary notice, Julian Bell was identified as 'the son of Mr. Clive Bell, the writer on art and literature'. That he also had a mother, a well-known painter, is unmentioned. Yet Vanessa Bell was the most important person in Julian's life, as in many ways he became in hers. During the anguished days following the shock of his death, Vanessa managed to scrawl pencilled notes in a notebook, dated only 'July 1937'. The remarkable, poignant entries start with the date of Julian's birth and appear like notes for a memoir, similar in intent but not form to the pictures of Julian towards the end of Virginia Woolf's memoir. It is almost as if Vanessa were trying in her pictorial way to keep the memories of Julian real in the agony of a suffering that led Virginia in her diary to liken the pains of childbirth to childdeath. (Vanessa characteristically apologised, Quentin Bell remembered, for not being stoical like Spanish mothers who were suffering as she was.)

Vanessa's memoir-sketches of Julian are in approximate chronological order. Their focus is on the relationship of mother and son. Virginia is not referred to, Quentin is mentioned mostly in relation to Julian, as is Angelica, and there is but one mention of Duncan Grant. Clive appears just twice. His grief is unmentioned in either memoir and there is only one reference to it in Virginia's diary. (Clive wrote in a letter how Julian's death was worse for Vanessa than himself because his life was more various; his regret, he said, was that Julian with his capacity for enjoyment had not experienced all the good things in life he might have.)

The relationship to Julian traced by Vanessa begins with confused feelings of love and pain – the joy of motherhood and the sense of her life being invaded. She then turns quickly to one of the central themes of her notes: how her relationship with Julian was complicated by the intrusions of nurses and governesses. Vanessa seems defensive in her memoir, and Julian – to use Leonard Woolf's term – appears rampageous, yet Vanessa is able to suggest how Julian's permissive upbringing resulted in his open honesty about his feelings. This is shown most clearly in Vanessa's joy that Julian could write to her of his going to bed with Anthony Blunt (a brief affair Virginia remained unaware of; Julian wrote to Vanessa that telling Virginia would be like putting an ad in *The Times*).

The difficulties of Julian's education and his mother's horror of schools make up another theme of Vanessa's memoir notes. Fragmentary sentence-sketches of Julian at home, in school and abroad break off with the first of his sustained love affairs at Cambridge. The largely empty notebook in which

Vanessa wrote suggests she may have intended to continue her memoir.

Vanessa's memoir never reaches the recent past that Virginia's memoir is mainly concerned with. China and Spain are not referred to. How she might have written of Julian in relation to them can be seen in an unpublished letter she wrote to Maynard Keynes a little later. Asking him to modify his King's College obituary remark on Julian's immaturity, Vanessa explained what Virginia had noticed – how Julian had changed while teaching in China. He now knew his own mind, knew the risks he was taking, and this was the only thing that reconciled Vanessa to his death (30th November 1937). Vanessa had written earlier to Julian just before he was killed how she wanted him to read the sane and unanswerable reply Keynes had just written in the *New Statesman and Nation* to Auden's poem 'Spain 1937'. Keynes had objected to the clash of ideologies in Auden's poem, replying to the famous phrase 'the conscious acceptance of guilt in the necessary murder' that murder did not settle moral issues. Although war could not always be avoided, Keynes was convinced that in Spain there should be peace at any price.

During the months in England before Julian's leaving for Spain, Vanessa also told Keynes in another unpublished letter that despite their terrible disagreement, she and Julian 'had an intimacy with each other greater in a way than any I have ever had with anyone else – and which could only have been possible with another grown up human being' (30th November 1937).

Vanessa Bell is not often regarded as a writer. Her reputation as Bloomsbury's matriarch immersed, as Virginia Woolf sometimes saw her, in the silent world of paint overlooks the evidence that Vanessa could write like the Stephen she was. That evidence is to be found in her letters and the dozen or so contributions she wrote over the years for The Memoir Club.

As she recovered from her grief, Vanessa turned from memoir to memorial. At her instigation a commemorative volume of Julian's poetry, letters and essays was planned that also included among other things Keynes's short obituary, some selective memoir notes by Julian himself, and the essay-letters on Roger Fry and to E.M. Forster. Quentin Bell edited *Essays, Poems and Letters* for the Hogarth Press, but he came to feel the disorganised book was hardly monumental. There was certainly nothing in it as moving as Vanessa's memoir, or Virginia's, except perhaps Julian's tribute to Vanessa in his poem 'Autobiography':

And one, my best, with such a calm of mind,
And, I have thought, with clear experience
Of what is felt of waste, confusion, pain,
Faced with a strong good sense, stubborn and plain;
Patient and sensitive, cynic and kind.

Before Vanessa could regain what Julian went on to describe as her 'sensuous mind' and 'lucid vision of form and colour and space', she was able to express in her memoir the waste, confusion and pain that Julian's death brought her.

Julian Bell's *Essays, Poems and Letters* was published the year following his death – 1938, the year of Munich and of three renowned Bloomsbury credos: E.M. Forster's early version of 'What I Believe', J.M. Keynes's Memoir Club paper 'My Early Beliefs' and Virginia Woolf's *Three Guineas*. Each in different ways can be regarded as a response to the ideas, feelings, and attitudes of Julian's generation that he articulated in his essays (as in a sadder way can Clive Bell's appeasement pamphlet of the same year, *War Mongers*). Together they provide a contemporary historical context in which the very private memoirs of both Virginia Woolf and Vanessa Bell may be read.

Memoir of Julian Bell (1937)

Friday July 30th 1937

I am going to set down very quickly what I remember about Julian, – partly because I am too dazed to write what I was writing; & then I am so composed that nothing is real unless I write it. And again, I know by this time what an odd effect Time has: it does not destroy people – for instance. I still think perhaps more truly than I did, of Roger [Fry], of Thoby [Stephen]: but it brushes away the actual personal presence.

The last time I saw Julian was at Clive's, two days before he went to Spain. It was a Sunday night, the beginning of June, a hot night. He was in his shirt sleeves. Lottie [Hope] was out, & we cooked dinner. He had a peculiar way of standing: his gestures were, as they say, characteristic. He made sharp quick movements, very sudden, considering how large & big he was, & oddly graceful. They reminded one of a sharp winged bird – one of the snipe here in the marsh. I remember his intent expression; seriously looking, I suppose at toast or eggs, through his spectacles. He had a very serious look: indeed he had grown much sterner since he came back from China. But of the talk I remember very little; except that by degrees it turned to politics. L.[Leonard] & Clive & Julian began to talk about Fascism, I daresay: & I remember thinking, now Clive is reining himself in with L.: being self restrained; which means there's trouble brewing. (I was wrong, as L. told me afterwards) Julian was now a grown man; I mean, he held his own with Clive & L.; & was cool & independent. I felt he had met many different kinds of people in China. Anyhow, as it was hot, & they talked politics, V. & A. [Vanessa & Angelica] & I went out into the Square, & then the others came, & we sat & talked. I remember saying something about Roger's papers, & telling Julian I shd.

leave them to him in my will. He said in his quick way, Better leave them to the British Museum. And I thought, thats because he thinks he may be killed. Of course we all knew that this was our last meeting – all together – before he went. But I had made up my mind to plunge into work, & seeing people, that summer. I had determined not to think about the risks, because, subconsciously I was sure he wd be killed: that is I had a couchant unexpressed certainty, from Thoby's death I think; a legacy of pessimism, which I have decided never to analyse. Then, as we walked toward the gate together, I went with Julian, & said, Wont you have time to write something in Spain? Wont you send it us? (This referred of course to my feeling, a very painful one, that I had treated his essay on Roger too lightly.) And he said, very quickly – he spoke quickly with a suddenness like his movements – 'Yes, I'll write something about Spain. And send it you if you like.' Do I said, & touched his hand. Then we went up to Clive's room: & then they went: we stood at the door to watch them. Julian was driving Nessa's car. At first it wdnt start. He sat there at the wheel frowning, looking very magnificent, in his shirt sleeves; with an expression as if he had made up his mind & were determined, tho' there was this obstacle – the car wdn't start. Then suddenly it jerked off – & he had his head thrown slightly back, as he drove up the Sqre. with Nessa beside him. Of course I noted it, as it might be our last meeting. What he said was, 'Goodbye until this time next year.'

We went in with Clive & drank. And talked about Julian. Clive & L. said that there was no more risk in going to Spain than in driving up & down to Charleston. Clive said that only one man had been hurt by a bomb. And he added, that Julian is very cool, like Cory [Bell] & myself. It's spirited of him to go, he added. I think I said, But it's a worry for Nessa. Then we discussed professions: Clive told us how Picasso had said, As a father, I'm so glad my son does not have one. And he said, he was glad Julian shd. be a 'character': he wd. always have eno' money to get bread & butter: it was a good thing he had no profession. He was a person who had no one gift in particular. He did not think he was born to be a writer – No he was a character, like Thoby. For some reason I did not answer, that he was like Thoby. I have always been foolish about that. I did not like any Bell to be like Thoby, partly through snobbishness, I suppose: nor do I think that Julian was like Thoby, except in the obvious way that he was young & very fine to look at. I said that Thoby had a natural style, & Julian had not.

In fact Julian was much rougher, more impulsive; more vigorous than Thoby. He had a strong element of the Bell in him. What do I mean? I think I mean that he was practical & caustic & shrewd; & then his extraordinary capacity for sex adventures, his readiness to go to bed with very ugly & rather commonplace young women was very unlike Thoby. He had much higher spirits. He was much more adapted to life. He was much less regularly beautiful to look at. But then he had a warmth, an impetuosity, that the Stephens dont have. Was it this that sometimes made me unfair to him? Some old jealousy? Or was it only the fear of an older generation for the younger: a fear that he did not respect our standards? – a jealousy for their canons of taste? But at the same time he was one of the most directly honest, & sharply & even sternly honest people I have ever known. He had too a very clear & strong intelligence. He was very Cambridge. He would wrinkle up his face in a very queer way, the Cambridge way. He would twist his hands. He would make the oddest grimaces. But what I think was very remarkable in him was his combination of extreme childishness, I mean irresponsibility, & gaiety & readiness for all sorts of love affairs, with his profound seriousness. He wrote to me from China about Ann [Stephen]: I'm glad you see that she's a really serious person. And then he laughed – less when he came back: but he laughed so that he broke chairs. 'My dear Aunt – Have you asked him what did you have for breakfast?' one of our stock jokes.

Now if I were able to develop this properly, I should say that the serious side had become much stronger in China. I felt it as I kissed him the afternoon he came here, the day after he got back. Perhaps I was shy. I think I felt he had taken his decision about Spain, & knew that I criticised it, on Nessa's account chiefly. There was something between us unsaid: something he was not going to let me say. He wd. not I think see me alone lest I should argue, or appeal to him. Our love of Nessa was I think the deepest union between us. He thought us much alike in some ways. He understood our intimacy. He felt that I resented the strain he had put on her.

There was also the damned literary question. I was always critical of his writing, partly I suspect from the usual generation jealousy; partly from my own enviousness of anyone who can do in writing what I cant do; & again (for I cant analyse out the other strains in a very complex feeling, roused partly by L.; for we envied Nessa I suspect for such a son; & there was L.'s family complex wh. made him eager, no, on the alert to criticise her children because he thought I admired them more than his family). I thought him very careless, not 'an artist', too personal in what he wrote, & 'all over the place'. This is the one thing I regret in our relationship: that I might have encouraged him more as a writer. But again thats my character; & I'm always forced, in spite of jealousy, to be honest in the end. Still this is my one regret; & I shall always have it; seeing how immensely generous he was to me about what I did – touchingly proud sometimes of my writing. But then I came to the stage 2 years ago of hating 'personality'; desiring anonymity; a complex state wh. I wd. one day have discussed with him. Then, I cd. not sympathise with wishing to be published. I thought it wrong from my new standpoint – a piece of the egomaniac, egocentric mania of the time. (For that reason I wd. not sign my Janet [Case] article.) But how cd. he know why I was so cool about publishing his things? Happily I made L. reconsider his poems, & we published them.

But I think he was grown very indifferent about literature; & perhaps a little bitter. I thought him bitter against [Stephen] Spender. I thought him a little jealous; & too caustic. One phrase I remember to Stephen at dinner – joining for the duration of the quarrel. I could be hurt sometimes by his rather caustic teasing, something like Clive's, & I felt it more because I have suffered from Clive's caustic & rather cruel teasing in the past. Julian had something of the same way of 'seeing through one'; but it was less personal, & stronger. That last supper party at Clive's I remember beginning a story about Desmond [MacCarthy]. It was about the L.S. [Leslie Stephen] lecture. I said Desmond took it very seriously as a compliment. And I cd. not remember who had had the L.S. lectureship, & said 'Didnt David [Cecil] do it?' & then Julian gave his flash of mockery & severity & said Ah how like you what you said – looking at Clive as tho' they both joined in suspecting my malice: in wh. he was that time wrong. But not always. I mean he had claws & cd. use them. He had feelings about the Bells. He thought I wanted to give pain, [he thought] me cruel, as Clive thinks me; but he told me, the night I talked to him before he went to China, that he never doubted the warmth of my feelings: that I suffered a great deal; that I had very strong affections.

But our relationship was perfectly secure because it was founded on our passion – not too strong a word for either of us – for Nessa. And it was this passion that made us both reserved when we met this last summer.

But what was the feeling that made him override this passion? Why had he changed? What was the reason why he went to Spain?

First there was the mere trivial cause: I think he was dissatisfied with his own standing among his generation. At least I felt he was jealous of Stephen etc. because they were published & praised; compared with them he was unknown. He had failed at Cambridge – I mean in the obvious things. That night with Sally Graves (in June or May last) we were arguing about education. I said poor old Eddie Playfair, marooned in the treasury. What a job to have! Julian said, I think he's much to be envied. I wish I'd been taught a job. No, it was all the old Bloomsbury view of education. I've only been taught to be a mere literary smattering. I interrupted & said Well I did my best to make you a barrister. You ought to have insisted, he said. And then told Sally that they ought to have been taught jobs. He told her she had the hard task of being a mother. He seemed bitter for a moment, & as if he regretted the Cambridge waste, & they agreed that they should have been taught to do something practical. I was so anxious to do everything to stop him from going that I got him to meet Kingsley Martin once at dinner, & then Stephen Spender, & so never saw him alone – except once, & then only for a short time. I had just come in with the Evening Standard in which The Years was extravagantly praised, much to my surprise. I felt very happy. It was a great relief. And I stood with the paper, hoping L. wd come & I cd tell him when the bell rang. I went to the top of the stairs, looked down, & saw Julian's great sun hat (he was amazingly careless of dress always – wd. come here with a tear in his trousers –) & I called out in a sepulchral voice 'Who is that?' Whereupon he started, & laughed & I let him in. And he said what a voice to hear or something light: then he came up; it was to ask for [Hugh] Dalton's telephone number. He stood there; I asked him to stay and see Leonard. He hesitated, but seemed to make up his mind that he must get on with the business of seeing Dalton. So I went & looked for the number. When I came back he was reading the Standard. I had left it with the review open. But he had turned, I think to the politics. I had half a mind to say, Look how I'm praised. And then I thought, No, I'm on the top of the wave: & its not kind to thrust that sort of thing upon people who aren't yet recognised. So I said nothing about it. But I wanted him to stay. And then again I felt, he's afraid I shall try to persuade him not to go. So all I said was, Look here Julian, if you ever want a meal, you've only to ring us up. Yes he said rather doubtingly, as if we might be too busy. So I insisted. We cant see too much of you. And followed him into the hall, & put my arm round him & said You cant think how nice it is having you back, & we half kissed; & he looked pleased & said Do you feel that? And I said yes, & it was as if he asked me to forgive him for all the worry; & then off he stumped, in his great hat & thick coat.

The last time I saw him & Nessa alone was at tea at the studio. That was after we had come back from France. I had tea alone with Nessa. The Chinese girl called. I went out & said Julian wdn't be back till 6. He was learning to drive a lorry. He had already put her off once. Then he came in. Again I think in his shirt sleeves. That time there was something formidable about him. Why? I dont know. I thought, again I'm only guessing, that he & Nessa had been arguing about Spain & that he had given way & was half angry with her for pressing him. (I had felt that at Rodmell, the day he came over with Bunny [David Garnett] just after his return, & he said If I'm late my mother (he only called her 'my mother' when he was humorous, or as now, ironical) will think I'm killed – from wh. I inferred that he half resented her anxiety about him – but for her, he'd have gone straight to the Intl [International] Brigade from Marseilles) But to return to the studio. I had again the feeling that he resented a woman's interfering with his plans. And since Nessa, rather nervously, had asked me to tell the Chinese girl to go away, & had not wished to ask her in to wait, I felt she was going against his wishes in this minute affair again; & since there had been so many arguments, he resented this interference too, & that was why she had asked me to do it. So now I said, I told her to go, & you'd be back at 6. And he was annoyed, & said severely, something about, As you've turned my friend away – & paid me no attention. This set my hackles up. An odd feeling. Half that I was a woman, & older, & wd. not stand rudeness from him. Anyhow I was silent. And he got up in the middle of something I was saying to Nessa, & walked about the room. Damned Cambridge insolence I said to myself. Then Nessa told him his map of the Channel had come. He sat down & unrolled it. Let me see, I said. And then he was interested, & showed me the currents, & I saw the wrecks of ships; & he told me that the very deep channel in the middle was the bed of an old river which had divided the land when England & France were joined. Then we smoothed out our grievance. I think he liked my standing up to him. I mean I think he felt that I wd. stand no nonsense, nor he either.

But this accentuates what I felt every time I met him after he came back – that he had changed: that he was no longer the high spirited irresponsible extravagant ridiculous boy who roared with laughter & threw himself back suddenly in a chair & then the middle of the chair broke – this he did without any apologies to my amusement to a chair just bought here – he was fixed, set; wd. stand no arguing, no persuasion, & yet I think was aware of something pigheaded, foolhardy, indefensible in his behaviour – something not silly, but rough, thoughtless, for so it was – his writing from Spain to Q. [Quentin Bell] to buy him maps, his giving Nessa that worry before he had come back. One morning I came in to L.'s room before lunch & Julian was there, to ask for some address I think; & I blurted out that I'd been seeing Stephen who said that S.M. [Spanish Medical]

Aid were completely disorganised, & there was no use in joining them. Whereupon he cut me short; waved it aside; & I shut up & said to myself well if he wont listen, there's nothing to be done. When he'd gone, L. & I agreed that argument was hopeless. One cd do nothing. Yet in fact when L. read him S's letters from Spain about Tony [Hyndman] & the way the Communists treated the Intl Brigade it decided him, Nessa says, not to go out as a soldier.

This impression of the change, for I had it so strongly I keep returning to it, was on me very markedly the first night he came back & we dined at Charleston & he wore his Chinese robes. Usually he wore any old shirt, shorts; all stained & torn. Now he was buttoned up in this straight long stiff silk robe, that fastened under his chin; a lilac robe I think; & he looked very beautiful; his small face at the top of the collar; clean shaven; very cleanly cut: his scar on the nose where he fell on the pencil holder as a baby; & the small very bright rather defiant eyes: but that night he looked of course unfamiliar; but composed, severe, rather frightening; & I was breaking my jokes against another surface; a harder surface; like an armour; except that now & then he was laughing again. But the robes made him very dignified, & smoothed out, & like a beech tree. The room was full of earrings & little jewels he had brought back for Angelica, Nessa & his loves. And he said to me I got you a glass fish. I saw it in the market & I said thats my dear Aunt – an old joke about the fish I used to give him to swim in his bath, because I liked them myself. He also gave me a little glass paper weight with flowers in it because it was the sort of thing I liked.

When I was in that horrid state of misery last summer with the proofs of The Years, in such misery that I cd. only work for 10 minutes & then go & lie down, I wrote to him my casual letter about his Roger paper, & he only answered many weeks later to say he had been hurt; so hadn't written; & then another letter of mine brought back the old family feeling. I was shocked at this, & wrote at once in time to catch him before he started home, to say dont let us ever quarrel about writing & I explained & apologised. All the same, for this reason, & because of his summer journey, & also because one always stops writing letters unless one has a regular day, we had one of those lapses in communication, which are bound to happen. I thought, when he comes back there'll be time to begin again. I thought he wd. get some political job & we should see a lot of him.

This lapse perhaps explains why I go on asking myself, without finding an answer, what did he feel about Spain? What made him feel it necessary, knowing as he did how it must torture Nessa to go? He knew her feeling. We discussed it before he went to China in the most intimate talk I ever had with him. I remember then he said how hard it was for her, now that Roger was dead; & that he was sorry that Quentin was so much at Charleston. He knew that: & yet deliberately inflicted this fearful anxiety on her. What made him do it? I suppose it's a fever in the blood of the younger generation which we cant possibly understand. I have never known anyone of my generation have that feeling about a war. We were all C.O.'s in the Great War. And tho' I understand that this is a 'cause', can be called the cause of liberty & so on, still my natural reaction is to fight intellectually: if I were any use, I should write against it: I should evolve some plan for fighting English tyranny. The moment force is used, it becomes meaningless & unreal to me. And I daresay he wd soon have lived through the active stage, & have found some other, administrative work. But that does not explain his determination. Perhaps it was restlessness, curiosity, some gift that never had been used in private life – & a conviction, part emotional, about Spain. Anyhow Q. said during one of our walks from the studio to T. Sqre. [Tavistock Square] 'If he hadn't gone he'd have been absolutely miserable,'

& said it with such conviction that I believe it. My own feeling then about his going wavers: I'm sometimes angry with him; yet feel it was fine, as all very strong feelings are fine; yet they are also wrong somehow: one must control feeling with reason. Quentin's way seems harder & finer; more considered; & also as I think a more effective measure, for I cant feel, when Janet [Vaughan] or Portia Holman talk of the encouragement Julian gave by his death, that they are right. They seem to me fire eaters; emotional; distorted in the way patriots are distorted by the emotional excitement of death, glory etc: all of which I detest, & think one shd. discount at all costs. These then are my varying feelings. But they come up against a rock in him, wh. I shall never understand, unless Nessa can explain it, or perhaps what Julian wrote & left with Quentin will explain it. Julian wd. have encouraged people more profoundly & importantly had he stayed in England & worked behind the scenes. Nevertheless I am conscious of some resentment with those, like [W.H.] Auden Spender & John [Lehmann], who do this: holding their views. This is personal tho': it comes from feeling why shd. we be made to suffer, & not their mothers?

Pictures of Julian at all stages, quite at random, & irrelevant – that is, without throwing light on his development – come to me: one night at Charleston when he suddenly began dancing in the Paddock with Angelica. She was a child then. He danced like a Russian, falling on one knee. It was extraordinarily beautiful; quite spontaneous, & unexpected & unconscious – in the evening of a hot day when we were sitting was it after dinner, on Q.'s birthday? or had they been acting? Another: this was when he was a child, 8 or 9, I shd. say. We had had a picnic at the bottom of the avenue that goes up behind Firle Park. We were packing up the tea things. He took a bottle of water & smashed it. He stood there in his knickerbockers with long naked legs looking defiant & triumphant. He smashed the bottle completely. The water or milk spread over the path. Mabel [Selwood] exclaimed Oh Julian. But he stood quite still smiling. I thought, This is the victorious male; now he feels himself the conqueror. It was a determined bold gesture, as tho' he wanted to express his own force & smiled at the consternation of the maids. Again: in the train going to Lewes with old Mrs. Uptn. & Mrs Harland, during the war. Mrs Up. & Mrs H. began talking about the downs. And Julian very exactly & eagerly explained that Firle Beacon was the highest of all the downs. He told them exactly how many feet it was in height. I was amused by the seriousness & eagerness with which he put them in possession of the true facts. Again: I was having breakfast in bed at Charleston. L. was in the north. J. brought me my tray & sat on the bed & talked to me about history. I think it was the F. Rev: & cross examined me; & I thought why haven't we a better history to teach the young? Then by Southease Church, he asked me very seriously to tell him the story of the Fr. Rev. I thought this is what really interests him – history. He was so eager, so precise, talking in that childish clear voice; mispronouncing certain words; but very exact; requiring precise answers. Perhaps it was that day I took Q. & J. into Southease Ch. and pretended to baptise them. He was very thin in those days, & used to screw his eyes & wrinkle his forehead. I asked him, do you like Asheham better than Charleston? He thought seriously & said, I like Asheham better, because of the rabbits. I remember taking him as a boy of 5 or 6 to tea at Buszards; & how he surprised me by being rather austere. He didn't care for cakes. He was rather severe; not greedy; rather scornful of luxury. I think this was always true of him. When he was at Cambridge I asked him if he ever drank too much. 'My friends arent that sort of people' he said. But this natural seriousness was always a surprise, mixed as it was with complete enjoyment of love; a mixture of Thoby's seriousness & Clive's jocundity:

very attractive. He never smoked, never even a cigarette I think. Nor was he any good at games, as far as I know. He had a passion though for machinery; I suppose. Roger I remember noted with amusement how he wd. spend a whole day dabbling with some toy in the pond. Like a small boy when he was grown up eno' to begin to be a proper schoolboy. Roger said this was a triumph for Nessa's method of educating her sons. They had never had any of the tastes of the ordinary schoolboy. They remained quite unconventional. Morgan [Forster] thought them rather too soft and childish. Why dont they run up to the top of Firle Beacon & get their fat down? he asked. But then he is oddly moral in some ways. Richard Braithwaite described him walking in the fields near Cambridge & 'throwing his great head back & snuffing the air' & how he thought he may be a great poet. Peter Lucas at one time too thought it possible that he might have real genius as a poet. I remember Julian telling me how once when he drove Desmond over here, Desmond suddenly said, 'And what are your views on life?' Julian was much amused, as if he cd. answer that when he was driving a car. He frightened Rd. Bte. [Richard Braithwaite] in that car: almost collided; grazed another car; going at full speed along the Eastbourne road. I suspect he was very brave & very rash as Q. said the other day. He had no sense of respectability or of manners in the ordinary sense. He was very rude to Lady Rhondda I remember, in the Cambridge way; but the Cambridge way was natural to him, not in the least an affectation. He went to his first Society dinner in evening dress. Desmond was amused. It was an odd thing to do, he thought. 'But he got over it with his natural Stephen charm.' I don't suppose J. noticed much one way or the other. He was entirely unself conscious: I doubt if he ever looked in the glass, or thought a moment about his clothes, or his appearance. Nessa used to mend his breeches. He was always patched, or in need of patching. And yet he had great sexual attraction & must have lived a great deal on love affairs – one after another – first that heavy beaver like woman Helen Suter [Soutar]: how cd. he see anything in her I wonder? Then Lettice [Ramsey]; another stout woman; but he liked her children, & had a great admiration for Frank Ramsey. Then there were many others: I always took it for granted he had some girl, & never thought he was seriously in love with any of them. But he was serious in his education of them. I remember Elizabeth Read – he at once took her education in hand, lectured her on philosophy, found out she wanted to write, lent her books, & wd. have gone to bed with her at once, had she not disappeared with her [Gilbert] Denny. Again, there was the mixture of seriousness & freedom. When he was at Cambridge, he said to me, I cant remember the words, how he thought Q. had had a woman; & Q. was younger than he was, & he had not yet had that experience. I remember his rather jealous worried way of asking me if I knew whether Q. had actually had a mistress in Paris, or Austria; & I felt that Julian was slightly perturbed, as if he had not yet taken the plunge, & thought that Q. had outdistanced him. This must have been when he first went up to Cambridge. He had a great respect for Q. He thought him a dark horse in some ways. He said, I think, that they very seldom talked about personal things. He admired Q.'s brains, & was interested in his Sussex activities – the Left Book Club meeting for instance: he said he must go & hear Q. speak.

JB (1931?)

J.B. discovered with a male siskin under a microscope.

JULIAN: God, I must hurry up and finish this poem, or John's will be out before mine. Well, I've done the head and the breast; now only the tail feathers and the claws remain. Reddish green, brown yellow, curled compact, close tail feathers elongated, bluish green, grey, umber, mealy white with spots of viscous ovoid cream. Rump red green gold, glaucous, chtion [?], transverse, barred.

GRACE: Please Mr Julian Mrs Woolf is downstairs and says would you stop making that noise.

JULIAN: Tell her I'm not making a noise. I'm writing poetry in the manner of Gerard Hopkins.

GRACE: Oh well she says the sound is so hideous she cant get on with her novel.

JULIAN: God bless the woman – her words have no sound; they've only got sense. Seepy, creaking, sweeping, with a creaking kind of beating of the penultimate dorsal jutting out femoral crepitational tail. The siskin whisking round the peeled off mouldy bottle green pear tree rivers. Well, I flatter myself that's a pretty good poem – all true to an inch. Anyhow nobody could say that was written by Virginia Woolf.

GRACE: Mrs Woolf says couldn't you try putting it all in one image, you'd find it shorter – and really she says if this noise goes on –

JULIAN: Put it all in one image? Oh well, perhaps that would be a good idea. I'm awfully pressed for time. The Hogarth Press is getting on with John's poems. He'll be reviewed before I am. He may get a column in the Times Lit Sup. So perhaps it would be a good idea to put the rest of the siskin into an image. But lord – what is an image? I cant remember. Where are my note books?

Image. No, I've got nothing under that heading. I'd better ring up Peter Lucas and ask him. Hello, Peter. I'm Julian. Can you tell me what an image is? Oh I see. But has any good poet ever used an image? Oh Shakespeare? Did I do Shakespeare for my tripos? Where are my note books. Yes I did him; Shakespeare's plays Lent term; Lord yes. There Shakespeare used fifty seven or possibly fifty eight different kinds of images. They may be classified under the following head – I say Peter, why dont we write a book and put Shakespeare's images under their proper headings with cross references. Let's make a note of that. I'll ask Chatto and Windus if they'd like six or seven volumes. But look here I'm in an awful pickle. Be a good chap and tell me if you think it would be all right to use one of Shakespeare's images in a poem in the manner of Gerard Hopkins on a dead siskin – male? You'll go to the University library and consult the authorities? Oh thanks but do look sharp. The siskin's been dead about a week – and John's book is coming out on Thursday and I'm awfully afraid Mr Blunden may review him in the Times Lit Sup. So I must get my image as quick as I can –

Well it looks as if I should have to make an image for myself. Now I dont think there's even time to make an image in the style of somebody else. Good Lord – I've never done such a thing in my life – think of writing in one's own style – think of making an image – I simply can't think how it's done. They generally begin like dont they – images. You say something's like something else. What the point of it is I can't conceive. A male siskin is a male siskin. Of course I can use my microscope and make a list of colours. But there isn't time. And that's not an image. Like like like – how can a thing be like anything else except the thing it is? And I might ring up Richard Braithwaite and ask what a thing is when it is a thing and not another thing and put that into poetry. I could do that. There'd be some sense in that. Like like like – well what did I have for lunch – cold beef – cold roast beef, cold salt roast beef. The siskin lies like – like cold salt roast beef the siskin lies. My word – that does it – that's an image – at least I suppose so. I'd better ring up Virginia and ask her. I say Virginia, is this an image – Like cold roast salt beef the whisking siskin

She's fainted.

Why did Clive ever marry into the Stephen family? That's at the bottom of it all – that's why I have to sit here writing poems about siskins when I really want to be shooting them. Now if only Clive had married Miss Hunt Grubb then I could have gone into parliament, and been a JP and never bothered my head about the writing of poetry in the manner of Gerard Hopkins. However I must get on with my poem. That'll do for the description in, in the manner of Gerard Hopkins. Now for the moral in the manner of Pope. And then a summing up in the manner of Richard Braithwaite, George Moore. There.

Hello Nessa. I wish you'd read this poem and tell me if you think it's exactly like every other poem that's ever been written? VANESSA: Well, Julian, it's no good asking me to read poetry, I stopped reading thirty five years ago, when I broke my spectacles. But why dont you ask your Aunt Virginia? I always ask Virginia about poetry. If she says it's good, I know it's bad, and if she says it's bad I know it's good. What does Virginia say about your poetry?

JULIAN: Oh it makes her faint.

VANESSA: Well then Julian you must be the very greatest poet in the English language.

Letters

Monk's House, Rodmell
June 28th 1936

My dearest Julian,

... So I read your thing on Roger only very slowly. I think it's full of idea; full of sharp insights; and there are a mass of things I would like to pilfer if I write [Roger Fry's biography], as I hope next autumn. My criticism is; first that you've not mastered the colloquial style, which is the hardest, so that it seemed to me (but my mind was weak) to be discursive, loose knit, and uneasy in its familiarities and conventions. However you could easily pull it together. Prose has to be tight, if it's not to smear one with mist. L. has read it and agrees with me on the whole. As Nessa may have told you, we can't use it as a letter [in The Hogarth Press Letters series], because it's too long; also, the letter series has proved a failure, and we have stopped it. What L. suggests is that it should be sent to [R.A.] Scott James of the Mercury, who might print it in two parts. Even so, I expect he would ask you to shorten it. I think the ideas were extremely interesting; I must go into them carefully. I wished there were more 'personality' but there's enough to give a hint of his relations with the younger generation. Thank goodness you'll be back before I've done anything that could be printed; so we can discuss it... I meant to add that I think you should shorten and condense before you print in a book: perhaps get rid of the letter form; and make it pure argument...

V

Dearest Virginia

Your name has been staring me in the face for a long time now from the list I keep of letters that I ought to write and don't, and I have been feeling rather guilty about it. The real reason, I suppose, was that I was rather hurt at your not liking my Roger better – which was most unreasonable of me, but I think your letter caught me just at the moment when one feels most sensitive about ones work, when its finished past altering and at the same time is still a part of oneself. Anyway, perhaps it was as well not to write to you then and to do so now, when it doesnt much matter to me, and when your [next] letter has just come and made me feel a due and proper familly affection for you....

Love,

Julian

Dearest Julian,

Your letter came this morning – the one in which you say that you didn't write because you were hurt that I didn't like your Roger better. I just send a line, though I doubt if you'll get it, to say how sorry I am – indeed angry with myself. The truth was I read your paper and wrote my letter when I was in a complete state of daze what with London proofs, and having headaches; I ought to have kept both for a clearer time; probably I expressed myself very badly and read very imperfectly. But all I want to say is that though I can't remember what I wrote, I certainly didn't mean to say anything that could possibly hurt you. Probably my impressions were mixed and incoherent; probably too you broached questions that I dont understand. But it is absurd to go over it at this distance of time – all I write to say is I'm very sorry.

… Don't for Gods sake let us quarrel about writings – yes, my book [*The Years*] is coming out. L. says it's no worse than the others…

Love from us both.

Virginia

Memoir Notes by Vanessa Bell (July 1937)

Feb. 4. 1908

When I first held him in my arms – the softness of his dark brown silky hair. All pain had become worth while.

Confused overwhelming feelings one did not understand.
Pain. Distress. Invasion of one's life.
Then danger to him & Knowledge of what I felt.

Sitting at a long window looking onto the square with him on my lap. Clive beside me – intense peace & joy. Painting him in his cradle every morning as he lay & kicked.
Drawing him as he began to stagger about – (I have those still)
Painting him as he sate each day in his chair by the window. (This I destroyed – oh why?)
Telling the hospital nurse at Seend I would never punish my child. Argument – she became angry & thought me foolish & ignorant. Making him laugh in the train going to Cornwall when he was 2 or 3 months old –
My life changed, invaded by this creature suddenly alive – My mornings half given to him, my evenings too – & Sunday mornings & one afternoon & evening a week.
His nurse a tyrant But what a strange intimacy.
Giving him my breast, not my nipple to suck when he was hungry & I too weak to keep him waiting & being so bitten by those hard gums – I had to hide the mark from the nurse for shame of my weakness
Going away when he was 6 months old – to Italy for a month or so – but I could hardly bear it
Playing in the Square

Being told by W.L. [Walter Lamb] that I ought to make him come & play beside me because he ought to do something to please me. But I was happy watching him by himself at the far side

Rushing upstairs terrified fetched by the maid as C [Clive] & I sate after tea 'Baby has run something into his eye' It was a sharp crayon holder, it had not gone into his eye, but near it – C fetched a doctor it had to be sewn up – Sudden relief from pain Only why had the nurse let him have such a thing. He could only just walk.

Trying to teach him to read at Asheham when he was 3 or 4 – but no – he would not. I gave it up –

Q's [Quentin's] arrival when he was 2? – End of this strange intense absorption – but a much more normal critical healthy attitude –

His jealousy of Q as a tiny baby. It did not last –

Q's long illness as a baby – I could think of nothing else – Then my own break down, being ill abroad & intense longing for them. Returning to the hot summer of 1911 –

Sitting in the garden at Guildford talking to R. [Roger Fry] & E.C. [Edward Carpenter] – He came, aged 3? & put a handful of gravel and earth all over my head & neck – R's astonishment that I did not scold him

Summers at Asheham –

Playing by a tub of water –

Summers before that at Studland. A lovely photograph of him naked on the beach – big & simple.

First wanting to know whether one could not know all that had happened by everyone's telling everyone all the way back to the beginning – I could only say yes –

When he was 2 we began to see R. constantly

Asheham – the War – when he was 6 – soldiers marching past along the road at the bottom –

London – air raids – I believe he was cross at not being taken out to see them but allowed to sleep –

1916 – Wissett. Sudden complete country freedom utter running wild – The garden in Spring – weeds – ducklings everything rampant. Mischief of all kinds. – Q. catching fish with his hand – Both in every <u>possible</u> scrape – I had too much to do & found myself speaking crossly –

London & Charleston. I divided between the two children at day school – Unendurable to me – So life at Charleston began at Christmas 1916 –

First Mabel [Selwood] as governess – D's [Duncan Grant's] painting of lessons in the garden –

Baths in the kitchen. Playing by the pond.

Tobogganing on the downs –

Attempt to co-educate with B-W. [Blanco-White] children.

His jealousy of them. Attacking them when out with Mabel – I told I must punish – Argument instead 'I cannot help feeling jealous & I would rather give way to my feelings of jealousy than control them.' What to say?

The B-W's had to go at the end of the term.

Visit from the MacC. [MacCarthy] children, who all fell into the pond. Happy together, all watching lightning one night sitting on their beds – His rage one day with M [Michael MacCarthy] – I saw him white with rage for some reason & had to interfere & console M –

Then Miss E [Edwards] as governess. Pretty, silly, intolerable, bullied by children – sent away in 6 weeks –

Then Mrs B [Brereton] – R's friend – At first a great relief – Her daughter Anne with her – 2 yrs older than J. She (Mrs B) seemed calm & sensible – aged about 50, had evidently had a passion for R – deserted by her husband etc. – wrote poems & stories for the Westminster Gazette –

Looking out of the sitting room window & seeing her dragging J to the front door while he rained blows on her face – Knowing I should not interfere but unable to resist rushing to the door – opening it. Sudden complete collapse of J. also of Mrs B – who was furious with me – She sent him to his room & I not allowed to go near him.

But I think I did later. Another time she punished him by shutting him in his & Q's bedroom. He got out of the window & escaped – General search discovered at last sitting calmly on a wall –

But on the whole not unsuccessful – though a stupid woman –

After a year A. [Angelica] was born – No servants. No nurse. General horror & misery – illness – absorption in A.

But gradual recovery. After 6 months move to London. Regent Sqre We had lived at Charleston 3 years – 1916–1919 –

Regent Sq – small rooms much too crowded – I & 3 children & nurse & cook.

Measles – J suddenly very ill – but quick recovery – Then to 50 Gordon Sq.

J at Owen's School – First day going to fetch him. Seeing him standing white – defiant – in a crowd of boys – 'Who is that?' 'My mother' very tense – afraid of the rough crowd round him – I walked up, & they were quite nice really – & said no more

One of those years, in London, while living at 50 [Gordon Square], I forgot his birthday till late in the day – it hurt him.

His & Q's shooting cats & (so they said) nearly hitting old gentlemen who complained to the police.

Tricks played by him & Mad Mary –

But first St. Tropez –
The autumn & winter J. taught by Mlle Bouvet who adored him & not Q. J played up to her so well. Lovely bathing & expeditioning with R.

Return to 46 [Gordon Square] – J to School at Leighton Park –
Saying good bye – 'You will have the others' 'But they are not you'

Boredom of school –
Worried about his feeling unable to work – Horror of all schools – but what could one do –

Then Paris for a year.

First equal talks – Friendship with Luce – Walking in Paris – Living with the Pinaults –

Cambridge – Lodgings First year perhaps ill at ease – No good rooming in London – only basement at 37 [Gordon Square] – Taking him to opera at Old Vic & finding he enjoyed it.
Then rooms at Cambridge & Cassis

Letters from him at Cassis telling me of his first love affair with A.B. [Anthony Blunt] Not a very real one – The joy of reading the letter as I walked down the field path & knew he meant to tell me things I had never expected it. I think his feeling for J. must have come first – but that had been stopped by her engagement – Then H.S. [Helen Soutar] Meeting her in his rooms – Very nice but oh dear – He had no illusions about her appearance – But they were happy – staying at Charleston – Jealousy on her part.
difficulties –

1. Back row, left to right: Angus Davidson, Duncan Grant, Julian Bell and Leonard Woolf. Front row, left to right: Virginia Woolf, Margaret Duckworth, and Clive and Vanessa Bell.

2. Virginia Stephen, Leslie Stephen.

II
Father and Aunts

Virginia Woolf's memoirs of her father and her aunts evoke the differing views that the platform of time offered her. The double vision of Leslie Stephen she noted in her diary, as a child condemning and a woman tolerating, is suggested in another way by two reminiscences that she was asked to write of him a quarter of a century apart.

The first was done in 1906 for F. W. Maitland's *The Life and Letters of Leslie Stephen*, which appeared two years after his death. The second was printed in *The Times* in 1932 on the centenary of Stephen's birth. The first memoir was anonymous – described by Maitland as 'what one of his daughters kindly allows me to repeat'. The second was headed 'Leslie Stephen, The Philosopher at Home, A Daughter's Memories, By Virginia Woolf'. Some of the differences in tone are what one might expect between an unknown, aspiring young writer and a famous, fifty-year-old author.

More significant, however, is the fact that these two memoirs are the only ones Virginia Woolf ever wrote for publication about her father. Her embodiments of Leslie Stephen in her first novel and most memorably in *To the Lighthouse* are fictive rather than factual. Her extended, disparaging account of him in the autobiographical letter to the infant Julian Bell was private and not written for publication. So were the diaries and letters that mention her father, as well as the more tolerant recollections of Stephen in the different versions of her unfinished 'Sketch of the Past'. The distinctions between public and private auto-biographical writing – so clear in Stephen's own works – and between novels and autobiographies are worth keeping in mind by readers concerned with truth as well as literary art.

Virginia Woolf's two published memoirs of her father shed light, however, on her other pictures of him in her fiction and her life writings. They do this by what is put in as well as what is left out. In the short memoir at the opening of the last chapter of

Maitland's biography of Leslie Stephen, Virginia begins with her memories as a child by charmingly describing how her father seemed almost a contemporary; only later would she come to feel more like Stephen's granddaughter. She then describes his reading to his children and his declaiming of poetry, the simplistic teaching of foreign languages that he tried to do after their mother's death, and finally his own reading towards the end of his life. Nothing critical is suggested here. (Maitland would not believe the family stories of Stephen's financial tantrums.)

For the longer *Times* centenary memoir, which Woolf did not initially want to do but was urged to by her sister and brother, she is more anecdotal, writing from a more distant temporal platform for readers who may have read *To the Lighthouse* but not the authorised *Life and Letters*. The ambivalence with which Woolf came to regard her father in 'Sketch of the Past' is now only implicit. In *The Times* she mentions Stephen's achievements, his mountaineering and the books he wrote (but not his editing of the *Dictionary of National Biography* referred to in the *Times* editorial note). The emphasis is domestic: on his dexterity with scissors and pen, his extraordinary memory for and love of poetry, his trenchant talk, his understatement and, when it came to money, his hyperbole.

In 'Sketch of the Past' Woolf distinguished three kinds of father: there was the writer father from whom, she says in *The Times*, she learned so much about writing and reading. There was the tyrant father that so preoccupies Woolf's commentators, and which Woolf suggests here in his financial anxieties. And then there was the sociable father, whose rather alarming sceptical silences have been overstressed, she thinks (perhaps by Anne Thackeray Ritchie among others). It is a grimmer Leslie Stephen who emerges from the centenary platform of her second memoir, puritanical yet unconventional, formidable yet unsatisfied with his achievements and suffering from the havoc that death wrought on his family, though Virginia Woolf only touches on this. And he emerges as a man whose values his daughter still honours and whose affections his friends cherished.

In 'The Leaning Tower', a late talk that she gave on writing, class and gender, Virginia Woolf referred again, but anonymously, to her father and what he had taught her. Urging her audience from the Workers' Educational Association to write freely for themselves as common readers and outsiders, she urged them to keep in mind 'a piece of advice that an eminent Victorian who was also an eminent pedestrian once gave to walkers: "Whenever you see a board up with 'Trespassers will be prosecuted', trespass at once."'

The last words Virginia Woolf wrote on Leslie Stephen were again private, but they suggest how she could reconcile the differing views of her father – and her mother – by stepping from the present platform of her diary to return to her childhood vision:

> How beautiful they were, those old people – I mean father & mother – how simple, how clear, how untroubled. I have been dipping into old letters & fathers memoirs. He loved her – oh & was so candid & reasonable & transparent – & had such a fastidious delicate mind, educated, & transparent. How serene & gay even their life reads to me: no mud; no whirlpools. And so human – with the children & the little hum & song of the nursery. But if I read as a contemporary I shall lose my childs vision & so must stop. Nothing turbulent; nothing involved: no introspection. (22nd December 1940)

After Leslie Stephen's death Virginia Woolf – still a Stephen – spent part of her time recuperating from a serious breakdown with Leslie's sister in Cambridge, while her brothers and sister moved to Bloomsbury. It was this aunt, Caroline Emelia Stephen

– an influential Quaker author – who suggested to Virginia that she help Maitland with his biography, making excerpts from his letters and eventually writing her daughter's impressions for the book. When Virginia began soon after to write sketches and reviews for the Church of England *Guardian* her aunt urged her to write history rather than journalism, never suspecting that perhaps her niece might write fiction. Virginia's last piece for the *Guardian* in 1909 was a short anonymous obituary of the distinguished woman who was her aunt.

The respectful, reticent memoir implies some personal acquaintance. Virginia emphasises Caroline's inspired faith, adding that 'she was no solitary mystic'. Her gift of expression, her common sense, her capacity for friendship, and her almost pathetic experience of suffering were all part of her influence, which extended to those who did not share her beliefs – one of whom was her obituarist. Even in her concise tribute, there is something of the ambivalence with which Virginia also regarded her aunt. Virginia complained in her letters that she was unable to say in her obituary what she thought, which was not respectful lamentation (12th April 1909). She admired the toughness of 'the Quaker' as she liked to call her, sometimes disagreeing entirely with her system of woolly benignity, and at other times finding her 'a very wise and witty old lady' (24th October 1904, July 1906).

What Caroline Emelia thought of her niece is suggested by her will. Virginia was left £2,500. (Virginia's siblings only received £100 apiece, but another niece, a Cambridge don, was left her much more valuable property.) Twenty years later Woolf mythologised her inheritance in *A Room of One's Own*. The narrator of that compound of fact and fiction is able to become a writer on the income of £500 a year (which £2,500 would not have yielded in 1909) from an aunt – hardly the valetudinarian Caroline – who fell off a horse in India.

Virginia Woolf's most important literary aunt, Anne Thackeray Ritchie, was the sister of her father's first wife. Novelist and memoirist, 'Aunt Anny' was for Leslie Stephen as well as his daughter an exciting contrast to the calming, if sometimes dampening, influence of Caroline Emelia and her visionary books. None of the three pieces that Virginia Woolf wrote on Lady Ritchie (as she became when her husband was knighted) are strictly speaking memoirs. Yet each is inevitably based on the sympathetic familiarity of a literary stepniece, as is the obituary that Leonard Woolf wrote for *The Times*, 28th February 1919, while Virginia was composing her tribute for the next week's *Times Literary Supplement*. Eight months later in *Night and Day*, her second novel, Virginia Woolf affectionately and amusingly reflected Anny's temperament in the sentimental, scatty yet shrewd character of Mrs Hilbery, who is forever trying and failing to write the biography of her famous poet father. Thackeray wanted no biography, so his daughter memorably evoked him in her many reminiscences and introductions to his works. Virginia's remarks on Anny's fiction are also an oblique commentary on the kind of novel she was writing in *Night and Day*.

Virginia Woolf's obituary tribute was preceded by a 1908 review of Anne Thackeray Ritchie's quasi-autobiographical essays *Blackstick Papers* and followed by a 1924 review of her letters. In the sixteen years that the articles span, Virginia Woolf developed from a novice reviewer into an established essayist and novelist. Yet her views of Aunt Anny from these different platforms of time are basically alike in their appreciation of her genius, her integrity as an artist, and the charm of her impressionistic prose with its unstructured yet discerning vividness and what Virginia called in the first review 'her flitting mockery'. Questions of sentimentality and cynicism raised by Thackeray's own work are touched on by Leonard Woolf in Anny's work, then rather dismissed by Virginia in her tribute. She thought she had done Anny very liberally, if 'a trifle rosily' she noted in her diary (5th March 1919). The last sentence with its birdsong of the soul's thanksgiving might be described that way.

The authoritative anonymity of the *TLS*'s summing up of Lady Ritchie's achievement allowed Virginia Woolf to quote her father on the perceptive humour and emotion of Anny's fitfully organised fiction. Anyone seeking the source of Leslie Stephen's quoted comments in 1919 would be frustrated, however, for they are taken – along with the repeated anecdote about the mixed-up chapters of her novel in Australia – from the unpublished autobiography *Mausoleum Book* Leslie left to his children. Leonard Woolf used it for his obituary as well, and Virginia did again in her review of Anny's letters. It seems appropriate that Virginia Woolf should rely on her father's memoir in writing of the daughter whose most enduring literary achievement may well have been the perpetuation of William Makepeace Thackeray's memory.

The review of Anne Thackeray Ritchie's letters is really about her memoirs, and here Virginia Woolf, now signing her name to her article, looks back into the Victorian period and into Anny's Bloomsbury childhood. It was those memoirs, as Virginia says in her tribute, that 'will be the unacknowledged source of much that remains in men's minds about the Victorian age' rather than 'the stout official biography' consecrated to great nine-teenth-century men, which Lytton Strachey had famously dismissed the year before in the ironic portraits of *Eminent Victorians*.

What influence Aunt Anny's admired reminiscences may have had on her stepniece's can be found in their humour rather than in their sentiment. (Her influence on the memoirs of another niece, Virginia Woolf's Bloomsbury friend Molly MacCarthy, seems more direct.) Virginia Woolf's memoirs do not praise the famous men she too knew in her own childhood. As she says at the unfinished end of 'Sketch of the Past', 'I cannot remember ever to have felt greatness since I was a child', yet her reviews of Henry James or George Meredith or Thomas Hardy are not reminiscences of their greatness but appreciative evaluations of their work.

Virginia Woolf's great aunt Julia Margaret Cameron died three years before her great niece was born, but she was familiar to Virginia Woolf from her mother's recollections, of course, as well as from Aunt Anny's reminiscences. And like Woolf's father, aunt and step-aunt, Julia Margaret Cameron left memorials of her work to be remembered by – not books this time, but the famous photographic portraits and group pictures.

Victorian Photographs of Famous Men and Fair Women was the mildly ironic title that the Woolfs gave to their 1924 Hogarth Press collection, which was the first major publication of these remarkable images. There were two introductions to the volume: Virginia Woolf's humorous life of Julia, collected here, and Roger Fry's discussion of the artistic originality with which she represented great Victorian male personalities and the conventionality with which she depicted the females. Her pictures of the famous men – among them Carlyle, Tennyson, Hershel, Darwin, Longfellow – were mostly hairy; those of the fair women largely vacuous. The indefinite focus of Mrs Cameron's lens and the slight blurring movements of the sitters brought out the hair and the vacuity. Among the exceptions were the striking portraits of Julia Cameron's niece, the widow Mrs Herbert Duckworth, before she remarried and became Virginia Woolf's mother. When the time came for the *Dictionary of National Biography* entry on Cameron, the editor turned to his wife, who wrote the entry, reprinted here, signing it with her initials and giving as its source 'personal knowledge'.

The influence of that knowledge on her daughter is suggested in the way Virginia Woolf illustrates the ardent, outspoken friendships and especially the 'persevering benevolence' of Aunt Julia that Julia Stephen describes. But Virginia had other sources, as her quotations indicate. Both Julia Margaret Cameron and 'poor Miss' Caroline Emelia Stephen figure in the memoirs of Anny Thackeray Ritchie. (Virginia Woolf's three memorialised aunts are all textually interconnected.) There were other sources: the autobiography of Henry Taylor that Julia Stephen had relied upon and the memoirs of Ethel Smyth, whose father relayed the wonderful but inaccurate opening anecdote of Virginia's memoir, a story repeated in a cousin's memoirs that Woolf had reviewed.

Julia Margaret Cameron's mid-nineteenth century milieu fascinated and appalled Virginia Woolf, and it stimulated some memorable remarks on Victorian letter writing in her introduction. (In preparation for writing it she asked Vanessa if she had any of Aunt Julia's profuse letters to their mother that she might quote.) Three years before she did her introduction to *Victorian Photographs of Famous Men and Fair Women*, Virginia wrote the comedy *Freshwater* based on Julia's circle at Freshwater on the Isle of Wight. Family and friends were to take part in it, Julia being played by Vanessa. Julia Margaret Cameron stayed in her stepniece's memory. Twelve years later Virginia Woolf rewrote and expanded the play for a private performance in Vanessa's London studio. The result of having family and friends acting as the Camerons, G.F. Watts, Ellen Terry, Tennyson and others produced the effect of something like a literary double exposure that superimposed modern Bloomsbury upon Victorian Freshwater.

A Daughter's Impressions (1906)

My impression as a child always was that my father was not very much older than we were. He used to take us to sail our boats in the Round Pond, and with his own hands fitted one out with masts and sails after the pattern of a Cornish lugger; and we knew that his interest was no 'grown-up' pretence; it was as genuine as our own; so there was a perfectly equal companionship between us. Every evening we spent an hour and a half in the drawing-room, and, as far back as I can remember, he found some way of amusing us himself. At first he drew pictures of animals as fast as we could demand them, or cut them out of paper with a pair of scissors. Then when we were old enough he spent the time in reading aloud to us. I cannot remember any book before *Tom Brown's School Days* and *Treasure Island*; but it must have been very soon that we attacked the first of that long line of red backs – the thirty-two volumes of the Waverley Novels, which provided reading for many years of evenings because when we had finished the last he was ready to begin the first over again. At the end of a volume my father always gravely asked our opinion as to its merits, and we were required to say which of the characters we liked best and why. I can remember his indignation when one of us preferred the hero to the far more life-like villain. My father always loved reading aloud, and of all books, I think, he loved Scott's the best. In the last years of his life, when he was tired of reading anything else, he would send one of us to the book-shelf to take down the first of the Waverley Novels that happened to present itself, and this he would open at random and read with quiet satisfaction till bedtime. He put *Guy Mannering* before most of the others because of Dandie Dinmont, whom he loved, and the first part of the *Heart of Midlothian* he admired so much that his reading of it cannot be forgotten. When my brothers had gone to school, he still went on reading to my sister and me, but chose more serious books. He read Carlyle's *French Revolution*, and stopped in the middle of *Vanity Fair*, because he said it was 'too terrible'. He read Miss Austen through, and Hawthorne and some of Shakespeare and many other classics. He began too to read poetry instead of prose on Sunday nights, and the Sunday poetry went on till the very end after the nightly reading had been given up.

His memory for poetry was wonderful; he could absorb a poem that he liked almost unconsciously from a single reading, and it amused him to discover what odd fragments and often quite second-rate pieces had 'stuck' to him, as he said, in this way. He had long ago acquired all the most famous poems of Wordsworth, Tennyson, Keats, and Matthew Arnold, among moderns. Milton of old writers was the one he knew best; he specially loved the 'Ode on the Nativity', which he said to us regularly on Christmas night. This was indeed the last poem he tried to say on the Christmas night before he died; he remembered the words, but was then too weak to speak them. He loved, too, and knew by heart since he had first read it, George Meredith's 'Love in the Valley', and he made us remark – and this was a rare instance of its kind – the beauty of Mr. Meredith's metres and his mastery over them. As a rule he disliked criticism of technical qualities, and, indeed, disliked being drawn into criticism of any kind. He often repeated, too, with enthusiasm, some of Sir Alfred Lyall's *Verses written in India*. His taste in poetry was very catholic, and if he liked a thing, it did not matter who had written it or whether the writer was unknown; it 'stuck' to him, and was added to his large store. He knew many of Mr. Rudyard Kipling's ballads by heart, and shouted Mr. Henry Newbolt's 'Admirals All' at the top of his voice as he went about the house or walked in Kensington Gardens, to the surprise of nursery-maids and park-keepers. The poets whose work he most cared to recite were, I think, Wordsworth, Tennyson and Matthew Arnold, whose 'Scholar Gipsey' was one of his greatest favourites. He very much disliked reading poems from a book, and if he could not speak from memory he generally refused to recite at all. His recitation, or whatever it may be called, gained immensely from this fact, for as he lay back in his chair and spoke the beautiful words with closed eyes, we felt that he was speaking not merely the words of Tennyson or Wordsworth but what he himself felt and knew. Thus many of the great English poems now seem to me inseparable from my father; I hear in them not only his voice, but in some sort his teaching and belief.

After my mother's death, my father was very anxious to take her place and to teach us as she had taught us, and for some years he gave up two of his precious morning hours to the drudgery of the schoolroom. Later on I read with him some Greek and some German. His method of teaching a language was always the same. He put all grammar on one side, and then, taking some classic, made straight for the sense. He once said that he owed Eton a grudge for not having made a scholar of him. In his last years he did not, I think, read any of the Greek or Latin classics by himself except his little *Plato*, which, being of a convenient size for his pocket, went with him on his journeys, and travelled to America and back. He read German, but seldom read it for pleasure, except Heine and Goethe. During his last illness he read French books by the score.

A Daughter's Memories (1932)

The philosopher at home

By the time that his children were growing up the great days of my father's life were over. His feats on the river and on the mountains had been won before they were born. Relics of them were to be found lying about the house – the silver cup on the study mantelpiece; the rusty alpenstocks that leant against the bookcase in the corner; and to the end of his days he would speak of great climbers and explorers with a peculiar mixture of admiration and envy. But his own years of activity were over, and my father had to content himself with pottering about the Swiss valleys or taking a stroll across the Cornish moors.

That to potter and to stroll meant more on his lips than on other people's is becoming obvious now that some of his friends have given their own version of those expeditions. He would start off after breakfast alone, or with one companion. Shortly before dinner he would return. If the walk had been successful, he would have out his great map and commemorate a new short-cut in red ink. And he was quite capable, it appears, of striding all day across the moors without speaking more than a word or two to his companion. By that time, too, he had written the *History of English Thought in the Eighteenth Century*, which is said by some to be his masterpiece; and the *Science of Ethics* – the book which interested him most; and *The Playground of Europe,* in which is to be found 'The Sunset on Mont Blanc' – in his opinion the best thing he ever wrote.

Chanted the poets

He still wrote daily and methodically, though never for long at a time. In London he wrote in the large room with three long windows at the top of the house. He wrote lying almost recumbent in a low rocking chair which he tipped to and fro as he wrote, like a cradle, and as he wrote he smoked a short clay pipe, and he scattered books round him in a circle. The thud of a book dropped on the floor could be heard in the room beneath. And often as he mounted the stairs to his study with his firm, regular tread he would burst, not into song, for he was entirely un-musical, but into a strange rhythmical chant, for verse of all kinds, both 'utter trash', as he called it, and the most sublime words of Milton and Wordsworth, stuck in his memory, and the act of walking or climbing seemed to inspire him to recite whichever it was that came upper most or suited his mood.

But it was his dexterity with his fingers that delighted his chil-dren before they could potter along the lanes at his heels or read his books. He would twist a sheet of paper beneath a pair of scissors and out would drop an elephant, a stag, or a monkey with trunks, horns, and tails delicately and exactly formed. Or, taking a pencil, he would draw beast after beast – an art that he practised almost unconsciously as he read, so that the fly-leaves of his books swarm with owls and donkeys as if to illustrate the 'Oh, you ass!' or 'Conceited dunce', that he was wont to scribble impatiently in the margin. Such brief comments, in which one may find the germ of the more temperate statements of his essays, recall some of the characteristics of his talk. He could be very silent, as his friends have testified. But his remarks, made suddenly in a low voice between the puffs of his pipe, were extremely effective. Sometimes with one word – but his one word was accompanied by a gesture of the hand – he would dispose of the tissue of exaggerations which his own sobriety seemed to provoke. 'There are 40,000,000 unmarried women in London alone!' Lady Ritchie once informed him. 'Oh, Annie, Annie!' my father exclaimed in tones of horrified but affectionate rebuke. But Lady Ritchie, as if she enjoyed being rebuked, would pile it up even higher next time she came.

Persons and places

The stories he told to amuse his children of adventures in the Alps – but accidents only happened, he would explain, if you were so foolish as to disobey your guides – or of those long walks, after one of which, from Cambridge to London on a hot day, 'I drank, I am sorry to say, rather more than was good for me,' were told very briefly, but with a curious power to impress the scene. The things that he did not say were always there in the background. So, too, though he seldom told anecdotes, and his memory for facts was bad, when he described a person – and he had known many people, both famous and obscure – he would convey exactly what he thought of him in two or three words. And what he thought might be the opposite of what other people thought. He had a way of upsetting established reputations and disregarding conventional values that could be disconcerting, and sometimes perhaps wounding, though no one was more respectful of any feeling that seemed to him genuine. But when, suddenly opening his bright blue eyes, and rousing himself from what had seemed complete abstraction, he gave his opinion, it was difficult to disregard it. It was a habit, especially when deafness made him unaware that this opinion could be heard, that had its inconveniences.

'I am the most easily bored of men', he wrote, truthfully as usual: and when, as was inevitable in a large family, some visitor threatened to stay not merely for tea but also for dinner, my father would express his anguish at first by twisting and untwisting a certain lock of hair. Then he would burst out, half to himself, half to the powers above, but quite audibly, 'Why can't he go? Why can't he go?' Yet such is the charm of simplicity – and did he not say, also truthfully, that 'bores are the salt of the earth'? – that the bores seldom went, or, if they did, forgave him and came again.

Too much, perhaps, has been said of his silence; too much stress has been laid upon his reserve. He loved clear thinking, he hated sentimentality and gush; but this by no means meant that he was cold and unemotional, perpetually critical and condemnatory in daily life. On the contrary, it was his power of feeling strongly and of expressing his feeling with vigour that made him sometimes so alarming as a companion. A lady, for instance, complained of the wet summer that was spoiling her tour in Cornwall. But to my father, though he never called himself a democrat, the rain meant that the corn was being laid; some poor man was being ruined; and the energy with which he expressed his sympathy – not with the lady – left her discomfited. He had something of the same respect for farmers and fishermen that he had for climbers and explorers. So, too, he talked little of patriotism, but during the South African War – and all wars were hateful to him – he lay awake thinking that he heard the guns on the battlefield. Again, neither his reason nor his cold common sense helped to convince him that a child could be late for dinner without having been maimed or killed in an accident. And not all his mathematics together with a bank balance which he insisted must be ample in the extreme, could persuade him, when it came to signing a cheque, that the whole family was not 'shooting Niagara to ruin', as he put it. The pictures that he would draw of old age and the Bankruptcy Court, of ruined men of letters who have to support large families in small houses at Wimbledon (he owned a very small house at Wimbledon) might have convinced those who complain of his understatements that hyperbole was well within his reach had he chosen.

A walk

Yet the unreasonable mood was superficial, as the rapidity with which it vanished would prove. The cheque-book was shut;

Wimbledon and the workhouse were forgotten. Some thought of a humorous kind made him chuckle. Taking his hat and his stick, calling for his dog and his daughter, he would stride off into Kensington Gardens, where he had walked as a little boy, where his brother Fitzjames and he had made beautiful bows to young Queen Victoria and she had swept them a curtsy, and so, round the Serpentine, to Hyde Park Corner, where he had once saluted the great Duke himself; and so home. He was not then in the least 'alarming'; he was very simple, very confiding; and his silence, though one might last unbroken from the Round Pond to the Marble Arch, was curiously full of meaning, as if he were thinking half aloud, about poetry and philosophy and people he had known.

He himself was the most abstemious of men. He smoked a pipe perpetually, but never a cigar. He wore his clothes until they were too shabby to be tolerable; and he held old-fashioned and rather Puritanical views as to the vice of luxury and the sin of idleness. The relations between parents and children today have a freedom that would have been impossible with my father. He expected a certain standard of behaviour, even, of ceremony, in family life. Yet if freedom means the right to think one's own thoughts and to follow one's own pursuits, then no one respected and indeed insisted upon freedom more completely than he did. His sons, with the exception of the Army and Navy, should follow whatever professions they chose; his daughters, though he cared little enough for the higher education of women, should have the same liberty. If at one moment he rebuked a daughter sharply for smoking a cigarette – smoking was not in his opinion a nice habit in the other sex – she had only to ask him if she might become a painter, and he assured her that so long as she took her work seriously he would give her all the help he could. He had no special love for painting; but he kept his word. Freedom of that sort was worth thousands of cigarettes.

Free of the library

It was the same with the perhaps more difficult problem of literature. Even today there may be parents who would doubt the wis-
dom of allowing a girl of fifteen the free run of a large and quite
unexpurgated library. But my father allowed it. There were certain facts – very briefly, very shyly he referred to them. Yet 'Read
what you like,' he said, and all his books, 'mangy and worthless',
as he called them, but certainly they were many and various, were
to be had without asking. To read what one liked because one
liked it, never to pretend to admire what one did not – that was
his only lesson in the art of reading. To write in the fewest possible
words, as clearly as possible, exactly what one meant – that was
his only lesson in the art of writing. All the rest must be learnt for
oneself. Yet a child must have been childish in the extreme not
to feel that such was the teaching of a man of great learning and
wide experience, though he would never impose his own views or
parade his own knowledge. For, as his tailor remarked when he
saw my father walk past his shop up Bond Street, 'There goes
a gentleman that wears good clothes without knowing it.'

In those last years, grown solitary and very deaf, he would
sometimes call himself a failure as a writer; he had been 'jack of
all trades, and master of none'. But whether he failed or succeeded as a writer, it is permissible to believe that he left a distinct
impression of himself on the minds of his friends. Meredith saw
him as 'Phoebus Apollo turned fasting friar' in his earlier days;
Thomas Hardy, years later, looked at the 'spare and desolate
figure' of the Schreckhorn and thought of

him,
Who scaled its horn with ventured life and limb,
Drawn on by vague imaginings, maybe,
Of semblance to his personality
In its quaint glooms, keen lights, and rugged trim.

But the praise he would have valued most, for though he was an agnostic nobody believed more profoundly in the worth of human relationships, was Meredith's tribute after his death: 'He was the one man to my knowledge worthy to have married your mother.' And Lowell, when he called him 'L.S., the most lovable of men', has best described the quality that makes him, after all these years, unforgettable.

Obituary (1909)

The death of Caroline Emelia Stephen will grieve many who knew her only from her writing. Her life had for years been that of an invalid, but she was wonderfully active in certain directions – she wrote, she saw her friends, she was able occasionally to read a paper to a religious society, until her final illness began some six weeks ago. Her books are known to a great number of readers, and it is not necessary here to dwell upon their contents. The *Service of the Poor* was published in 1871, *Quaker Strongholds* in 1890, *The First Sir James Stephen* in 1906, and *Light Arising* in 1908. A few words as to her life and character may interest those who had not the happiness of knowing her personally. She was born in 1834, and was the daughter of Sir James Stephen, Under-Secretary for the Colonies, and of his wife, Jane Catherine Venn, daughter of the Rector of Clapham. She was educated, after the fashion of the time, by masters and governesses, but the influence which affected her most, no doubt, was that of her father, always revered by her, and of her home, with its strong Evangelical traditions. Attendance upon her mother during her last long illness injured her health so seriously that she never fully recovered. From that date (1875) she was often on the sofa, and was never again able to lead a perfectly active life. But those who have read her *Quaker Strongholds* will remember that the great change of her life took place at about this time, when, after feeling that she 'could not conscientiously join in the Church of England Service' she found herself 'one never-to-be-forgotten Sunday morning… one of a small company of silent worshippers'. In the preface to that book she has described something of what the change meant to her; her written and spoken words, her entire life in after-years, were testimony to the complete satisfaction it brought her.

Her life was marked by little outward change. She lived at Malvern for some time, but moved in 1895 to Cambridge, where she spent the last years of her life in a little cottage surrounded by a garden. But the secret of her influence and of the deep impression she made even upon those who did not think as she did was that her faith inspired all that she did and said. One could not be with her without feeling that after suffering and thought she had come to dwell apart, among the 'things which are unseen and eternal' and that it was her perpetual wish to make others share her peace. But she was no solitary mystic. She was one of the few to whom the gift of expression is given together with the need of it, and in addition to a wonderful command of language she had a scrupulous wish to use it accurately. Thus her effect upon people is scarcely yet to be decided, and must have reached many to whom her books are unknown. Together with her profound belief she had a robust common sense and a practical ability which seemed to show that with health and opportunity she might have ruled and organised. She had all her life enjoyed many intimate friendships, and the dignity and charm of her presence, the quaint humour which played over her talk, drew to her during her last years many to whom her relationship was almost maternal. Indeed, many of those who mourn her to-day will remember her in that aspect, remembering the long hours of talk in her room with the windows opening on to the garden, her interest in their lives and in her own, remembering, too, something tender and almost pathetic about her which drew their love as well as their respect. The last years of her life among her flowers and with young people round her seemed to end fittingly a life which had about it the harmony of a large design.

Blackstick Papers: Essays (1908)

Sir Richard Jebb spoke once of Lady Ritchie's 'fairy-like way of viewing life', and fitly enough she invokes the good Fairy Blackstick to preside over the fresh collection of her papers, *Blackstick Papers*. They deal with 'certain things in which she was interested – old books, young people, schools of practical instruction, rings, roses, sentimental affairs, &c.' But the fairy does more than preside; we are convinced, as we read, that she inspires too. Again and again we put the book down, and exclaim that it is impossible to define the charm, or refer it, as the critic should, to some recognised source. It is far simpler to ascribe it to magic, and to leave it to the spirits themselves to say what magic is. It is true that Lady Ritchie makes use of many things that are not in the least supernatural; she picks up an old book about Haydn, or a new book about George Sand; she stays at a place like Brighton, where we may all stay for ourselves if we wish it. We know the kind of treatment which such themes receive generally at the hands of the essayists; they are learned, prosaic, or sentimental. But Lady Ritchie is none of these things. If we try to discover what her method is we must imagine that she looks out of a window, takes somehow the impression of a gay, amusing world, turns over the leaves of her book and seizes a sentence here and there, remembers something that happened forty years ago, and rounds it all into an essay which has the buoyancy and the shifting colours of a bubble in the sun. The genuine nature of her magic is proved by the truth of much that seems almost too good to be true; she snatches a figure from the past, and shows as George Sand 'a sort of sphinx in a black silk dress. Her black hair shone dully in the light as she sat motionless; her eyes were fire; it was a dark face, a dark figure in the front of a theatre box.' Nor is she invariably kind. Comparing modern women with their mothers, she says – 'They may be authors, but they are not such authorities; they may be teachers, but they are no longer mistresses.' We must remember, when we talk of fairies and magic, that the best of them are not purely visionary, but see something more in common things than we do, and have rather a different standard to judge them by. Lady Ritchie will surprise us again and again by her flitting mockery. It is for this reason that we are so little conscious of the fact that by far the greater part of her book is devoted to the past and dead people – Haydn, Tourgénieff, Bewick, the Misses Berry. There is 'a vivid and innocent brightness', to quote Sir Richard again, in her view, so that the past itself wears cheerful colours. It seems sometimes that she is more at home in the earlier days, when people were upright, smiling, and discreet, than in the present; the words of Horace Walpole lie in perfect harmony upon her page, and we imagine that the great ladies of the eighteenth century had something of the manner of her prose. But to praise good breeding is an impertinence; it will be better to quote one passage, and so to give what analysis fails to give.

The stately old tree falls, and we miss its spreading shade and comprehending shelter; to the last the birds have sung for us in the branches and the leaves hang on to the end, and old and young gather round still, and find rest and entertainment until the hour comes when all is over. The old branches go, and the ancient stem with so many names and signs carved deep in its bark, and the memories of the storms and sunshines of nearly a century.

Tribute: Lady Ritchie (1919)

The death of Lady Ritchie will lead many people to ask themselves what she has written, or at least which of her books they have read; for she was never, or perhaps only as Miss Thackeray for a few years in the 'sixties and 'seventies of the last century, a popular writer. And, unless we are mistaken, they will find themselves, on taking down *The Story of Elizabeth* or *Old Kensington*, faced with one of those curious problems which are more fruitful and more interesting than the questions which admit of only one answer. The first impression of such a reader will be one of surprise, and then, as he reads on, one of growing perplexity. How is it possible, he will ask, that a writer capable of such wit, such fantasy, marked by such a distinct and delightful personality, is not at least as famous as Mrs Gaskell, or as popular as Anthony Trollope? How has she escaped notice all these years? And by what incredible oversight have we allowed passages which can only be matched in the classics of English fiction to be so hidden beneath the modern flood that the sight of them surprises like the flash of a jewel in a dust heap? What are the faults that have neutralised – if they have neutralised – this astonishing bounty of nature?

Some of the reasons at any rate for this neglect are not far to seek, and are to be ascribed more to the fault of the public than to the fault of the writer. Lady Ritchie was incapable of much that appears necessary to ensure popularity. She wrote neither for the busy man who wants to be diverted, nor for the earnest who wishes to be instructed; she offered neither sensation nor impropriety, and her beauty and distinction of manner were as unfailing as they were natural. Such characteristics are not those that appeal to a large public; and, indeed her gifts and her failings were so curiously and so provokingly combined that, while none of her novels can be called a masterpiece, each one is indisputably the work of a writer of genius. But the test of the masterpiece is not, after all, the only test. We can also ask ourselves whether a novelist has created a world which, with all its limitations, is still a habitable place, and a place which but for him would never have come into existence. Now Lady Ritchie's novels and recollections, although it is only honest to admit that they have their lapses, their unbridged abysses and their tracts of obscurity, offer us a world unlike any other when we are setting out upon one of our voyages of the imagination. We doubt whether since the death of George Eliot in 1880 the same can be said of the work of any other Englishwoman. It is not only still possible to read with enjoyment *The Story of Elizabeth*, *The Village on the Cliff*, and *Old Kensington*, but as we read them we have the sense that there is nothing quite like them in existence. When we remember that they were published in 1866, 1865, and 1873 respectively, we may feel certain that they owe their survival to some real, and to some extremely rare, magic of their own.

We should ascribe it largely to their absolute individuality. Some writers, like Charlotte Brontë, triumph by means of one overwhelming gift; others, like George Borrow, are so queerly adjusted to the world that their vision reveals a new aspect of things; but Lady Ritchie's genius belonged to neither of these classes. It would be difficult to quote any scene in her books as one of surpassing power, or to claim that the reading of her writing has influenced our view of life one way or the other. On the other hand she possessed indisputably what seems to be as rare a gift as any – the gift of an entirely personal vision of life, of which her books are the more or less complete embodiment. She had her own sense of character, of conduct, of what amused her, of what delighted her eye, of trees and flowers and the beauty of the seasons. She was completely and transparently faithful to her vision. In other words she was a true artist; and when once we have said that of any writer we have to draw back a little and look at his work as a whole, with the understanding that whether great art or lesser art it is a thing unique of its kind.

With every excuse for taking shelter behind the great shield of tradition inherited from her father, nothing impresses one more in Lady Ritchie's work than the certainty that every stroke proceeded directly from her own hand; a more natural gift than hers never existed. It came to her directly, and owed nothing to discipline or to the painstaking study of other writers. Not many novelists can have assumed as early as she did complete command not only of their own method, but of their own language. *The Story of Elizabeth*, written in early youth, is as fluent, easy and composed in style as the work of one who has been framing sentences and casting scenes for a lifetime. This early maturity was the result of a great natural gift growing up with all the most polished tools at command in an atmosphere forbidding any but the most sensitive right use of them. Thus endowed, and thus wisely cherished, she rested we will not say indolently, but frankly and simply in her gift. She trusted to her instinct and her instinct served her well. Young writers might do worse than go to Lady Ritchie's pages for an example of the power of an apparently simple and yet inevitably right sense of the use of language. There is no premeditation, no effort at profundity; her prose appears to swim and float through the air rather than to march firmly with its feet set upon the ground. But every sentence is formed; they cohere together; and invariably at the end of a chapter or paragraph there is a sense that the melody has found its way through one variation and another to its natural close. The impression, it may be of the slightest, has been conveyed to us; the scene, it may be of the most transient, lives with the breath of life. She has, in fact, done exquisitely and exactly what she set out to do.

However this was achieved, and her instinct after all was a highly cultivated instinct, no one can read *Old Kensington* or *The Story of Elizabeth* without being aware of a certain spaciousness and composure of manner which are oddly unlike the style of the present time. The style, of course, corresponds to something in the point of view. Her heroes and heroines live in a world of their own, which is not quite our world, but a rather simpler and more dignified place. They do not analyse themselves very much, nor do they complicate their lot by taking upon them the burden of public right and wrong. They are blissfully unconscious even of themselves. Much that a modern writer would dissect into detail is presented to us in the mass. One might suppose that the process of building up such a character as Dolly Vanborough in *Old Kensington* was a simple one calling only for a few strokes of the brush in comparison with the process by which some of our complex young women are now constructed. And yet Dolly Vanborough lives, and the others for the most part merely serve to tell the time of day like efficient little clocks whose machinery will soon be out of order. Like all true creations, Dolly Vanborough and Elly Gilmour, while they pay homage to the conventions of their time have within them capacities for feelings which are never called forth by the story. We could fancy ourselves at ease today with one of these honest, arch, rather reserved young ladies in spite of the fact that she wears a crinoline and has no sort of desire for a vote. Against all probability, indeed, the thing we should find strange in them is not their sentimentality or their extravagance of feeling, but rather their slight hardness of heart, their determination to keep always well within the bounds of common sense.

Here, indeed, lay one of the paradoxes and fascinations of Lady Ritchie's art. With all her power of creating an atmosphere of tremulous shadows and opal tinted lights, with all her delight in the idyllic and the rapturous, the shapes of things are quite hard underneath and have, indeed, some surprisingly sharp edges. It would be as superficial to sum her up as a sentimentalist as it was to call her father a cynic. In her case the sentiment is more hopefully and openly expressed, but her sight is singularly clear; the shrewd, witty judgement of a woman of the world smiles constantly upon her own rosy prospects. It is notable that she had neither heroes nor heroines in the accepted sense of those terms; her hero is generally a clumsy, ineffective young man who spends too much and fails to pass his examinations; and the heroine, even the first born of all, has a thousand follies of a natural human kind. Who, after all, had a greater delight than Lady Ritchie in the delineation of a fool – a delight naturally without a trace of cruelty? We need only recall the inimitable Mrs Palmer, whose mother had been an Alderville, 'and the Aldervilles are all young and beautiful, helpless, stout, and elegantly dressed'. As an example of her vein of humour, here is a little scene from *Old Kensington*:

'Hulloh!' shouted Sir Thomas, as he drove out at the park-gates. 'Look there, Anley! he is draining Medmere, and there is a new window to the schools. By jove!'

'Foolish young man!' said Mr Anley, 'wasting his substance, draining cottages, and lighting school rooms!' and he looked out with some interest.

'Then, Uncle Jonah, you are foolish yourself,' said Bell.

'Are you turned philanthropist, Uncle Jonah?' said Mrs Boswarrick. 'I wish someone would take me and Alfred up. What have you been doing?'

'I make it a rule never to do anything at the time that can be put off till the morrow,' said Mr Anley apologetically. 'My cottages were tumbling down, my dear, so I was obliged to prop them up.'

'He bought them from papa,' said Bell. 'I can't think why.'

'It is all very well for bachelors like you and Raban to amuse yourselves with rebuilding,' said Sir Thomas, joining in from his box in an aggravated tone; 'if you were a married man, Anley, with a wife and daughters and milliners' bills, you would see how much was left at the end of the year for improvements.'

'To hear the talk, one oughtn't to exist at all,' says Mrs Boswarrick, with a laugh.

Or if we want to confute a charge of undue sentimentality we can point to characters like Robert Henley and Rhoda, into whose shallow depths and twisted motives Lady Ritchie's art strikes like a beam of the sun.

But many fine talents have come to grief over the novel, which demands precisely those qualities of concentration and logical construction in which Lady Ritchie was most naturally or wilfully deficient. We could guess, if we had not good authority for knowing, that in composing her novels 'she wrote fragments as thoughts struck her and pinned them (with literal not metaphor pins) at parts of her manuscript till it became a chaotic jumble maddening to the printers'. As Leslie Stephen, one of her warmest admirers, wrote of her –

She showed more perception and humour, more delicate and tender and beautiful emotion, than would have made the fortune of a dozen novelists, had she had her faculties more in hand. Had she, for example, had any share of Miss Austen's gift for clearness, proportion, and neatness, her books would have been much better, as incomparably more successful.

It is true the string does not always unite the pearls; but the pearls are there, in tantalising abundance – descriptions, sketches of character, wise and profound sayings, beyond the reach of any but a few modern writers, and well able to stand the ordeal of printing together in some book of selections.

But the qualities which militated against her success as a novelist did not stand in her way in another branch of literature in which she excelled. The lack of ambition, the childlike candour of mind which had so much rather praise and exalt than weigh and ponder made her singularly happy in her task, or pleasure, of recording the great and small figures of her own past. Here the whimsical and capricious genius has its scope unfettered and exquisitely inspired. We should be inclined to put her at the head of all modern artists in this manner and to claim for her indeed, that she invented an art of her own. For her method is quite unlike the ordinary method. There is no analysis, no criticism, and few good stories – or the stories only become good in the telling. But her skill in suggesting the mood, the spirit, the look of places and people defies any attempt to explain it. How, we ask, from such apparently slight materials are such vivid impressions created? Here is Charlotte Brontë:

My father, who had been walking up and down the room, goes out into the hall to meet his guests; then, after a moment's delay, the door opens wide, and the two gentlemen come in leading a tiny, delicate, serious, little lady, pale, with fair straight hair and steady eyes. She may be a little over thirty; she is dressed in a little barège dress with a pattern of faint green moss. She enters in mittens, in silence, in seriousness; our hearts are beating with wild excitement.

Trelawny:

Not very long afterwards came a different visitor, still belonging to that same company of people. I had thrown open the dining-room door and come in looking for something, and then I stopped short, for the room was not empty. A striking and somewhat alarming-looking person stood alone by the fireplace with folded arms; a dark impressive looking man, not tall, but broad and brown and weather beaten, gazing with a sort of scowl at his own reflection in the glass. As I entered he turned slowly and looked at me over his shoulder. This was Trelawny, who had come to see my father. He frowned, walked deliberately and slowly from the room, and I saw him no more.

George Sand:

> She was a stout middle-aged woman, dressed in a stiff watered-silk dress, with a huge cameo, such as people then wore, at her throat. Her black shiny hair shone like polished ebony, she had a heavy red face, marked brows, great dark eyes; there was something – how shall I say it? – rather fierce, defiant, and set in her appearance, powerful, sulky; she frightened one a little. 'That is George Sand,' said Mrs Sartoris, bending her head and making a friendly sign to the lady with her eye-glasses. The figure also bent its head, but I don't remember any smile or change of that fixed expression.

We feel that we have been in the same room with the people she describes. Very likely the great man has said nothing memorable, perhaps he has not even spoken: occasionally her memory is not of seeing him but of missing him: never mind – there was an ink-pot, perhaps a chair, he stood in this way, he held his hat just so, and miraculously and indubitably there is before our eyes. Again and again it has happened to us to trace down our conception of one of the great figures of the past not to the stout official biography consecrated to him, but to some little hint or fact or fancy dropped lightly by Lady Ritchie in passing, as a bird alights on a branch, picks off the fruit and leaves the husk for another.

Something of the kind will perhaps be her destiny in the future. She will be the unacknowledged source of much that remains in men's minds about the Victorian age. She will be the transparent medium through which we behold the dead. We shall see them lit up by her tender and radiant glow. Above all and for ever she will be the companion and interpreter of her father, whose spirit she has made to walk among us not only because she wrote of him, but because even more wonderfully she lived in him. It would have pleased her well to claim no separate lot for herself, but to be merged in the greater light of his memory. Praise of her own work would have seemed to her unnecessary. It would have surprised her, but it would have pleased her, to realise with what a benediction many are today turning to the thought of her, thanking her not only for her work, but thanking her more profoundly for the bountiful and magnanimous nature, in which all tender and enchanting things seemed to grow – a garden, one might call it, where the airs blew sweetly and freely and the bird of the soul raised an unpremeditated song of thanksgiving for the life that it had found so good.

Obituary by Leonard Woolf (1919)

DEATH OF LADY RITCHIE
THACKERAY'S DAUGHTER

We regret to announce the death on Wednesday [26th February], at the Porch, Freshwater, of Lady Ritchie, widow of Sir Richmond Ritchie and daughter of William Makepeace Thackeray.

When a near relation of some famous man of a former generation dies, it is customary to say that a link with the past has been broken: Lady Ritchie's death is the breaking of such a link, and much more. One cannot think of her merely as the daughter of Thackeray, because she was one of those rare examples, a child of a great writer inheriting much of her parent's genius. Though not many novel readers of this generation take down Miss Thackeray's *Old Kensington* from the mid-Victorian bookshelf, yet if they do, they will see at once that there is no exaggeration in applying the word 'genius' to its author. But if she deserved more fame and success than she achieved as a novelist, it was rather in her life and personality that the wayward spirit of genius showed itself.

The bare chronicle of her life was placid and, on the whole, singularly happy. She was born in 1837, the great novelist's eldest child. Before her sixth year, owing to Mrs Thackeray's mental breakdown, her father's marriage had become, as he described it, 'a wreck'. This fact profoundly influenced her early years. She and her sister, the only two children who survived, were sent to live at Paris with Thackeray's mother, who had married Major Smyth, the original of Colonel Newcome. In 1846 their father brought them back to live with him in the house in York Street, Kensington, where *Vanity Fair* was written. Lady Ritchie's books show clearly how these two homes, Paris and Kensington, divided and dominated her childhood. She lived, if one may use the expression, that chapter of the Apocrypha which praises famous men. Thackeray himself gave his two small daughters a companionship and intimacy which are usually impossible between parents and children, middle-age and childhood. And in Paris and Kensington almost every famous man and woman of the time came into their lives. Lady Ritchie herself in *Chapters From Some Memoirs* has made their figures live for us with astonishing vividness like the procession of our own fireside memories of the past; the dying Chopin playing in his bare and narrow room to the grim Scotch spinster who brought him the basket of food; Count D'Orsay sitting at the breakfast table and seeming 'to fill the bow-window with radiance as if he were Apollo'; Samuel Rogers 'standing in the middle of the room, taking leave of his hostess, nodding his head... a little like a Chinese mandarin with an ivory face'. As the children grew up there came the Carlyles and Dickens and Leech and Charlotte Brontë and George Eliot and Mrs Kemble and Kingsley, and a whole host of greater and lesser lights. So they lived among famous men until their father's death in 1863, and, indeed, after it. There was an extraordinarily strong affection between the two sisters, so strong that they were not separated by the marriage of the younger to Leslie Stephen in 1867. Miss Thackeray herself, in 1877, married her cousin, the late Sir Richmond Ritchie, by whom she had a son and a daughter.

Lady Ritchie published her first book, *The Story of Elizabeth*, in 1863, and this was followed during the next twenty-two years by six other novels or volumes of stories. But she will probably be best remembered by her reminiscences. It was in that form of writing that her genius found its most suitable material. She had the rare power of not only feeling, but also of making others feel, how amusing and romantic her fireside memories were. *Old Kensington* is the best of her novels, because in it she is allowing this power full play, not in the world of facts, but of imagination. And the very qualities of her genius left her without that laborious concentration necessary for the production of so massive a work of art as the novel. Her manuscripts, made up of hastily written fragments pinned confusedly together, were the despair of her friends and publishers, and once when one of her novels was published in Australia the last chapter was printed in the middle of the book and nobody found it out. That fact shows her limitations more clearly than any criticism. She had her father's sentiment and shrewdness so admirably and so contradictorily combined that she continually verged on his besetting sins of sentimentality and cynicism and never fell into either; she had poetry and a lightness of wit and humour that made her conversation inimitable; and, lastly, she had that quality which made one of her severest friends say that she was the most sympathetic person he had ever met. But she never possessed that sense of facts, order, continuity, without which the production of a great work of art is impossible. Her mind was too quick and too light for the heavier and slower world in which she had to live. In conversation she fascinated and amused all who knew her, and yet what she said never seemed quite to fit in with what others were saying; it was, someone once remarked, as though she were singing her own beautiful but erratic tune just outside the circle of the other musicians.

Lady Ritchie was left a widow in 1912. Among various writings in which she commemorated her father, there should not be forgotten her contributions to the centenary edition of Thackeray's works; they contained, besides introductions which only his daughter could have written, a good many pieces unfinished or unpublished before.

The Enchanted Organ: Letters (1924)

The enormous respectability of Bloomsbury was broken one fine morning about 1840 by the sound of an organ and by the sight of a little girl who had escaped from her nurse and was dancing to the music. The child was Thackeray's elder daughter, Anne. For the rest of her long life, through war and peace, calamity and prosperity, Miss Thackeray, or Mrs Richmond Ritchie, or Lady Ritchie, was always escaping from the Victorian gloom and dancing to the strains of her own enchanted organ. The music, at once so queer and so sweet, so merry and so plaintive, so dignified and so fantastical, is to be heard very distinctly on every page of the present volume.

For Lady Ritchie was incapable at any stage of her career of striking an attitude or hiding a feeling. The guns are firing from Cremorne for the taking of Sebastopol, and there she sits scribbling brilliant nonsense in her diary about 'matches and fairy tales'. 'Brother Tomkins at the Oratory is starving and thrashing himself because he thinks it is right,' and Miss Thackeray is reading novels on Sunday morning 'because I do not think it is wrong'. As for religion and her grandmother's miseries and the clergyman's exhortations to follow 'the one true way', all she knows is that it is her business to love her father and grandmother, and for the rest she supposes characteristically 'that everybody is right and nobody knows anything'.

Seen through this temperament, at once so buoyant and so keen, the gloom of that famous age dissolves in an iridescent mist which lifts entirely to display radiant prospects of glittering spring, or clings to the monstrous shoulders of its prophets in many-tinted shreds. There are Mr FitzGerald and Mr Spedding coming to dinner 'as kind and queer and melancholy as men could be'; and Mrs Norton 'looking like a beautiful slow sphinx'; and Arthur Prinsep riding in Rotten Row with violets in his buttonhole – '"I like your violets very much", said I, and of course they were instantly presented to me' – and Carlyle vociferating that a cheesemite might as well understand a cow as we human mites our maker's secrets; and George Eliot, with her steady little eyes, enunciating a prodigious sentence about building one's cottage in a valley, and the power of influence, and respecting one's work, which breaks off in the middle; and Herbert Spencer stopping a Beethoven sonata with 'Thank you, I'm getting flushed'; and Ruskin asserting that 'if you can draw a strawberry you can draw anything'; and Mrs Cameron paddling about in cold water till two in the morning; and Jowett's four young men looking at photographs and sipping tumblers of brandy and water until at last 'poor Miss Stephen', who has been transplanted to an island where 'everybody is either a genius, or a poet, or a painter, or peculiar in some way', ejaculates in despair, 'Is there *nobody* commonplace?'

'Poor Miss Stephen', bored and bewildered, staying with several cousins at the hotel, represented presumably the Puritanical conscience of the nineteenth century when confronted by a group of people who were obviously happy but not obviously bad. On the next page, however, Miss Stephen is significantly 'strolling about in the moonlight'; on the next she has deserted her cousins, left the hotel, and is staying with the Thackerays in the centre of infection. The most ingrained Philistine could not remain bored, though bewildered she might be, by Miss Thackeray's charm. For it was a charm extremely difficult to analyse. She said things that no human being could possibly mean; yet she meant them. She lost trains, mixed names, confused numbers, driving up to Down, for example, precisely a week before she was expected, and making Charles Darwin laugh – 'I can't for the life of me help laughing,' he apologised. But then if she had gone on the right day, poor Mr Darwin would have been dying. So with her writing, too. Her novel

Angelica 'went off suddenly to Australia with her feet foremost, and the proofs all wrong and the end first!!!' But somehow nobody in Australia found out. Fortune rewarded the generous trust she put in it. But if her random ways were charming, who, on the other hand, could be more practical or see things when she liked more precisely as they were? Old Carlyle was a god on one side of his face, but a 'crossgrained, ungrateful, self-absorbed old nutcracker' on the other. Her most typical, and, indeed, inimitable sentences rope together a handful of swiftly gathered opposites. To embrace oddities and produce a charming, laughing harmony from incongruities was her genius in life and in letters. 'I have just ordered,' she writes, 'two shillings' worth of poetry for [my fisherman]... We take little walks together, and he carries his shrimps and talks quite enchantingly.' She pays the old dropsical woman's fare in the omnibus, and in return the 'nice jolly nun hung with crucifixes' escorts her across the road. Nun and fisherman and dropsical old woman had never till that moment, one feels sure, realised their own charm or the gaiety of existence. She was a mistress of phrases which exalt and define and set people in the midst of a comedy. With Nature, too, her gift was equally happy. She would glance out of the window of a Brighton lodging-house and say: 'The sky was like a divine parrot's breast, just now, with a deep, deep, flapping sea.' As life drew on, with its deaths and its wars, her profound instinct for happiness had to exert itself to gild those grim faces golden, but it succeeded. Even Lord Kitchener and Lord Roberts and the South African War shine transmuted. As for the homelier objects which she preferred, the birds and the downs and the old charwoman 'who has been an old angel, without wings, alas! and only a bad leg', and the smut-black chimney-sweeps, who were 'probably gods in disguise', they never cease to the very end to glow and twinkle with merriment in her pages. For she was no visionary. Her happiness was a domestic flame, tried by many sorrows. And the music to which she dances, frail and fantastic, but true and distinct, will sound on outside our formidable residences when all the brass bands of literature have (let us hope) blared themselves to perdition.

Introduction (1926)

Julia Margaret Cameron, the third daughter of James Pattle of the Bengal Civil Service, was born on June 11, 1815. Her father was a gentleman of marked, but doubtful, reputation, who after living a riotous life and earning the title of 'the biggest liar in India', finally drank himself to death and was consigned to a cask of rum to await shipment to England. The cask was stood outside the widow's bedroom door. In the middle of the night she heard a violent explosion, rushed out, and found her husband, having burst the lid off the coffin, bolt upright menacing her in death as he had menaced her in life. 'The shock sent her off her head then and there, poor thing, and she died raving.' It is the father of Miss Ethel Smyth who tells the story (*Impressions that Remained*), and he goes on to say that, after 'Jim Blazes' had been nailed down again and shipped off, the sailors drank the liquor in which the body was preserved, 'and, by Jove, the rum ran out and got alight and set the ship on fire! And while they were trying to extinguish the flames she ran on a rock, blew up, and drifted ashore just below Hooghly. And what do you think the sailors said? "That Pattle had been such a scamp that the devil wouldn't let him go out of India!"'

His daughter inherited a strain of that indomitable vitality. If her father was famous for his lies, Mrs Cameron had a gift of ardent speech and picturesque behaviour which has impressed itself upon the calm pages of Victorian biography. But it was from her mother, presumably, that she inherited her love of beauty and her distaste for the cold and formal conventions of English society. For the sensitive lady whom the sight of her husband's body had killed was a Frenchwoman by birth. She was the daughter of Chevalier Antoine de l'Étang, one of Marie

Antoinette's pages, who had been with the Queen in prison till her death, and was only saved by his own youth from the guillotine. With his wife, who had been one of the Queen's ladies, he was exiled to India, and it is at Ghazipur, with the miniature that Marie Antoinette gave him laid upon his breast, that he lies buried.

But the de l'Étangs brought from France a gift of greater value than the miniature of the unhappy Queen. Old Madame de l'Étang was extremely handsome. Her daughter, Mrs Pattle, was lovely. Six of Mrs Pattle's seven daughters were even more lovely than she was. 'Lady Eastnor is one of the handsomest women I ever saw in any country,' wrote Henry Greville of the youngest, Virginia. She underwent the usual fate of early Victorian beauty: was mobbed in the streets, celebrated in odes, and even made the subject of a paper in *Punch* by Thackeray, 'On a good-looking lady'. It did not matter that the sisters had been brought up by their French grandmother in household lore rather than in book learning. 'They were artistic in their finger tips, with an appreciation – almost to be called a culte – for beauty.' In India their conquests were many, and when they married and settled in England, they had the art of making round them, whether at Freshwater or at Little Holland House, a society of their own ('Pattledom' it was christened by Sir Henry Taylor), where they could drape and arrange, pull down and build up, and carry on life in a high-handed and adventurous way which painters and writers and even serious men of affairs found much to their liking. 'Little Holland House, where Mr Watts lived, seemed to me a paradise,' wrote Ellen Terry, 'where only beautiful things were allowed to come. All the women were graceful, and all the men were gifted.' There, in the many rooms of the old Dower House, Mrs Prinsep lodged Watts and Burne-Jones, and entertained innumerable friends among lawns and trees which seemed deep in the country, though the traffic of Hyde Park Corner was only two miles distant. Whatever they did, whether in the cause of religion or of friendship, was done enthusiastically.

Was a room too dark for a friend? Mrs Cameron would have a window built instantly to catch the sun. Was the surplice of the Rev. C. Beanlands only passably clean? Mrs Prinsep would set up a laundry in her own house and wash the entire linen of the clergy of St Michael's at her own expense. Then when relations interfered, and begged her to control her extravagance, she nodded her head with its coquettish white curls obediently, heaved a sigh of relief as her counsellors left her, and flew to the writing-table to despatch telegram after telegram to her sisters describing the visit. 'Certainly no one could restrain the Pattles but themselves,' says Lady Troubridge. Once indeed the gentle Mr Watts was known to lose his temper. He found two little girls, the granddaughters of Mrs Prinsep, shouting at each other with their ears stopped so that they could hear no voices but their own. Then he delivered a lecture upon self-will, the vice, he said, which they had inherited from their French ancestress, Madame de l'Étang. 'You will grow up imperious women,' he told them, 'if you are not careful.' Had they not into the bargain an ancestor who blew the lid off his coffin?

Certainly Julia Margaret Cameron had grown up an imperious woman; but she was without her sisters' beauty. In the trio where, as they said, Lady Somers was Beauty, and Mrs Prinsep Dash, Mrs Cameron was undoubtedly Talent.

'She seemed in herself to epitomise all the qualities of a remarkable family,' wrote Mrs Watts, 'presenting them in a doubly distilled form. She doubled the generosity of the most generous of the sisters, and the impulsiveness of the most impulsive. If they were enthusiastic, she was so twice over; if they were persuasive, she was invincible. She had remarkably fine eyes, that flashed like her sayings, and grew soft and tender if she was moved...' But to a child (*Memories and Reflections by Lady Troubridge*, p. 34) she was a terrifying apparition 'short and squat, with none of the Pattle grace and beauty about her, though more than her share of their passionate energy and wilfulness. Dressed in dark clothes, stained with chemicals from her photography (and smelling of them too), with a plump eager face and a voice husky, and a little harsh, yet in some way compelling and even charming,' she dashed out of the studio at Dimbola, attached heavy swans' wings to the children's shoulders, and bade them 'Stand there' and play the part of the Angels of the Nativity leaning over the ramparts of Heaven.

But the photography and the swans' wings were still in the far future. For many years her energy and her creative powers poured themselves into family life and social duties. She had married, in 1838, a very distinguished man, Charles Hay Cameron, 'a Benthamite jurist and philosopher of great learning and ability', who held the place, previously filled by Lord Macaulay, of fourth Member of Council at Calcutta. In the absence of the Governor-General's wife, Mrs Cameron was at the head of European society in India, and it was this, in Sir Henry Taylor's opinion, that encouraged her in her contempt for the ways of the world when they returned to England. She had little respect, at any rate, for the conventions of Putney. She called her butler peremptorily 'Man'. Dressed in robes of flowing red velvet, she walked with her friends, stirring a cup of tea as she walked, halfway to the railway station in hot summer weather. There was no eccentricity that she would not have dared on their behalf, no sacrifice that she would not have made to procure a few more minutes of their society. Sir Henry and Lady Taylor suffered the extreme fury of her affection. Indian shawls, turquoise bracelets, inlaid portfolios, ivory elephants, 'etc.', showered on their heads. She lavished upon them letters six sheets long 'all about ourselves'. Rebuffed for a moment, 'she told Alice [Lady Taylor] that before the year was out she would love her like a sister', and before the year was out Lady Taylor could hardly imagine what life had been without Mrs Cameron. The Taylors loved her; Aubrey de Vere loved her; Lady Monteagle loved her; and 'even Lord Monteagle, who likes eccentricity in no other form, likes her'. It was impossible, they found, not to love that 'genial, ardent, and generous' woman, who had 'a power of loving which I have never seen exceeded, and an equal determination to be loved'. If it was impossible to reject her affection, it was even dangerous to reject her shawls. Either she would burn them, she threatened, then and there, or, if the gift were returned, she would sell it, buy with the proceeds a very expensive invalid sofa, and present it to the Putney Hospital for Incurables with an inscription which said, much to the surprise of Lady Taylor, when she chanced upon it, that it was the gift of Lady Taylor herself. It was better, on the whole, to bow the shoulder and submit to the shawl.

Meanwhile she was seeking some more permanent expression of her abundant energies in literature. She translated from the German, wrote poetry, and finished enough of a novel to make Sir Henry Taylor very nervous lest he should be called upon to read the whole of it. Volume after volume was despatched through the penny post. She wrote letters till the postman left, and then she began her postscripts. She sent the gardener after the postman, the gardener's boy after the gardener, the donkey galloping all the way to Yarmouth after the gardener's boy. Sitting at Wandsworth Station she wrote page after page to Alfred Tennyson until 'as I was folding your letter came the screams of the train, and then the yells of the porters with the threat that the train would not wait for me', so that she had to thrust the document into strange hands and run down the steps. Every day she wrote to Henry Taylor, and every day he answered her.

Very little remains of this enormous daily volubility. The Victorian age killed the art of letter writing by kindness: it was only too easy to catch the post. A lady sitting down at her desk a hundred years before had not only certain ideals of logic and restraint before her, but the knowledge that a letter which cost so much money to send and excited so much interest to receive was worth time and trouble. With Ruskin and Carlyle in power, a penny post to stimulate, a gardener, a gardener's boy, and a galloping donkey to catch up the overflow of inspiration, restraint was unnecessary and emotion more to a lady's credit, perhaps, than common sense. Thus to dip into the private letters of the Victorian age is to be immersed in the joys and sorrows of enormous families, to share their whooping coughs and colds and misadventures, day by day, indeed hour by hour. The standard of family affection was very high. Illness elicited showers of enquiries and kindnesses. The weather was watched anxiously to see whether Richard would be wet at Cheltenham, or Jane catch cold at Broadstairs. Grave misdemeanours on the part of the governesses, cooks, and doctors ('he is guilty of culpable carelessness, profound ignorance', Mrs Cameron would say of the family physician), were detailed profusely, and the least departure from family morality was vigilantly pounced upon and volubly imparted.

Mrs Cameron's letters were formed upon this model; she counselled and exhorted and enquired after the health of dearest Emily with the best; but her correspondents were often men of exalted genius to whom she could express the more romantic side of her nature. To Tennyson she dwelt upon the beauty of Mrs Hambro,

> frolicsome and graceful as a kitten and having the form and eye of an antelope... Then her complexion (or rather her skin) is faultless – it is like the leaf of 'that consummate

flower' the Magnolia – a flower which is, I think, so mysterious in its beauty as if it were the only thing left unsoiled and
unspoiled from the garden of Eden... We had a standard
Magnolia tree in our garden at Sheen, and on a still summer
night the moon would beam down upon those ripe rich vases,
and they used to send forth a scent which made the soul faint
with a sense of the luxury of the world of flowers.

From such sentences it is easy to see why Sir Henry Taylor
looked forward to reading her novel with dread. 'Her genius (of
which she has a great deal) is too profuse and redundant, not
distinguishing between felicitous and infelicitous,' he wrote.
'She lives upon superlatives as upon her daily bread.'

But the zenith of Mrs Cameron's career was at hand. In 1860
the Camerons bought two or three rose-covered cottages at
Freshwater, ran them together, and supplemented them with
outhouses to receive the overflow of their hospitality. For at
Dimbola – the name was taken from Mr Cameron's estate in
Ceylon – everybody was welcome. 'Conventionalities had no
place in it.' Mrs Cameron would invite a family met on the
steamer to lunch without asking their names, would ask a
hatless tourist met on the cliff to come in and choose himself
a hat, would adopt an Irish beggar woman and send her child
to school with her own children. 'What will become of her?'
Henry Taylor asked, but comforted himself with the reflection
that though Julia Cameron and her sisters 'have more of hope
than of reason', still 'the humanities are stronger in them than
the sentimentalities', and they generally brought their eccentric
undertakings to a successful end. In fact the Irish beggar child
grew up into a beautiful woman, became Mrs Cameron's parlourmaid, sat for her portrait, was sought in marriage by a rich
man's son, filled the position with dignity and competence, and
in 1878 enjoyed an income of two thousand four hundred

pounds a year. Gradually the cottages took colour and shape under Mrs Cameron's hands. A little theatre was built where the young people acted. On fine nights they trapesed up to the Tennysons and danced; if it were stormy, and Mrs Cameron preferred the storm to the calm, she paced the beach and sent for Tennyson to come and pace by her side. The colour of the clothes she wore, the glitter and hospitality of the household she ruled reminded visitors of the East. But if there was an element of 'feudal familiarity', there was also a sense of 'feudal discipline'. Mrs Cameron was extremely outspoken. She could be highly despotic. 'If ever you fall into temptation,' she said to a cousin, 'down on your knees and think of Aunt Julia.' She was caustic and candid of tongue. She chased Tennyson into his tower vociferating 'Coward! Coward!' and thus forced him to be vaccinated. She had her hates as well as her loves, and alternated in spirits 'between the seventh heaven and the bottomless pit'. There were visitors who found her company agitating, so odd and bold were her methods of conversation, while the variety and brilliance of the society she collected round her caused a certain 'poor Miss Stephen' to lament: 'Is there nobody commonplace?' as she saw Jowett's four young men drinking brandy and water, heard Tennyson reciting 'Maud', while Mr Cameron wearing a coned hat, a veil, and several coats paced the lawn which his wife in a fit of enthusiasm had created during the night.

In 1865, when she was fifty, her son's gift of a camera gave her at last an outlet for the energies which she had dissipated in poetry and fiction and doing up houses and concocting curries and entertaining her friends. Now she became a photographer. All her sensibility was expressed, and, what was perhaps more to the purpose, controlled in the new born art. The coal-house was turned into a dark room; the fowl-house was turned into a glass-house. Boatmen were turned into King Arthur; village girls into Queen Guenevere. Tennyson was wrapped in rugs: Sir Henry Taylor was crowned with tinsel. The parlourmaid sat for her portrait and the guest had to answer the bell. 'I worked fruitlessly but not hopelessly,' Mrs Cameron wrote of this time. Indeed, she was indefatigable. 'She used to say that in her photography a hundred negatives were destroyed before she achieved one good result; her object being to overcome realism by diminishing just in the least degree the precision of the focus. Like a tigress where her children were concerned, she was as magnificently uncompromising about her art. Brown stains appeared on her hands, and the smell of chemicals mixed with the scent of the sweet briar in the road outside her house. She cared nothing for the miseries of her sitters nor for their rank. The carpenter and the Crown Prince of Prussia alike must sit as still as stones in the attitudes she chose, in the draperies she arranged, for as long as she wished. She cared nothing for her own labours and failures and exhaustion. 'I longed to arrest all the beauty that came before me, and at length the longing was satisfied,' she wrote. Painters praised her art; writers marvelled at the character her portraits revealed. She herself blazed up at length into satisfaction with her own creations. 'It is a sacred blessing which has attended my photography,' she wrote. 'It gives pleasure to millions.' She lavished her photographs upon her friends and relations, hung them in railway waiting-rooms, and offered them, it is said, to porters in default of small change.

Old Mr Cameron meanwhile retired more and more frequently to the comparative privacy of his bedroom. He had no taste for society himself, but endured it, as he endured all his wife's vagaries, with philosophy and affection. 'Julia is slicing up Ceylon,' he would say, when she embarked on another adventure or extravagance. Her hospitalities and the failure of the coffee crop ('Charles speaks to me of the flower of the coffee plant. I tell him that the eyes of the first grandchild should be more beautiful than any flowers,' she said) had brought his affairs into a precarious state. But it was not business anxieties alone that made Mr Cameron wish to visit Ceylon. The old philosopher became more and more obsessed with the desire to return to the East. There was peace; there was warmth; there were the monkeys and the elephants whom he had once lived among 'as a friend and a brother'. Suddenly, for the secret had been kept from their friends, the Camerons announced that they were going to visit their sons in Ceylon. Their preparations were made and friends went to say good-bye to them at Southampton. Two coffins preceded them on board packed with glass and china, in case coffins should be unprocurable in the East; the old philosopher with his bright fixed eyes and his beard 'dipt in moonlight' held in one hand his ivory staff and in the other Lady Tennyson's parting gift of a pink rose; while Mrs Cameron, 'grave and valiant,' vociferated her final injunctions and controlled not only innumerable packages but a cow.

They reached Ceylon safely, and in her gratitude Mrs Cameron raised a subscription to present the Captain with a harmonium. Their house at Kalutara was so surrounded by trees that rabbits and squirrels and minah birds passed in and out while a beautiful tame stag kept guard at the open door. Marianne North, the traveller, visited them there and found old Mr Cameron in a state of perfect happiness, reciting poetry, walking up and down the verandah, with his long white hair flowing over his shoulders, and his ivory staff held in his hand. Within doors Mrs Cameron still photographed. The walls were covered with magnificent pictures which tumbled over the tables and chairs and mixed in picturesque confusion with books and draperies. Mrs Cameron at once made up her mind that she would photograph her visitor and for three days was in a fever of excitement. 'She made me stand with spiky coconut branches running into my head… and told me to look perfectly natural,' Miss North remarked. The same methods and ideals ruled in Ceylon that had once ruled in Freshwater. A gardener was kept, though there was no garden and the man had never heard of the existence of such a thing, for the excellent reason that Mrs Cameron thought his back 'absolutely superb'. And when Miss North incautiously admired a wonderful grass green shawl that Mrs Cameron was wearing, she seized a pair of scissors, and saying: 'Yes, that would just suit you,' cut it in half from corner to corner and made her share it. At length, it was time for Miss North to go. But still Mrs Cameron could not bear that her friends should leave her. As at Putney she had gone with them stirring her tea as she walked, so now at Kalutara she and her whole household must escort her guest down the hill to wait for the coach at midnight. Two years later (in 1879) she died. The birds were fluttering in and out of the open door; the photographs were tumbling over the tables; and, lying before a large open window Mrs Cameron saw the stars shining, breathed the one word 'Beautiful,' and so died.

Biography by Julia Prinsep Stephen (1886)

CAMERON, JULIA MARGARET (1815–1879), photographer, born at Calcutta on 11 June 1815, was the third daughter of James Pattle of the Bengal civil service. In 1838 she married John Hay Cameron, then member of the law commission in Calcutta. Her other sisters married General Colin Mackenzie, Henry Thoby Prinsep, Dr. Jackson, M.D., Henry Vincent Bayley, judge of the supreme court of Calcutta and the nephew of Henry Vincent Bayley, Earl Somers, and John Warrender Dalrymple of the Bengal civil service. Miss Pattle was well known in Calcutta society for her brilliant conversation. She showed her philanthropy in 1846, when through her energy and influence she was able to raise a considerable sum for the relief of the sufferers in the Irish famine. Mrs Cameron came to England with her husband and family in 1848. They resided in London and afterwards went to Putney, and in 1860 settled at Freshwater in the Isle of Wight, where they were the neighbours and friends of Lord Tennyson. In 1875 they went to Ceylon; they visited England in 1878, and returned to Ceylon where she died on 26 Jan. 1879.

Mrs Cameron was known and beloved by a large circle of friends. She corresponded with Wordsworth, she was well known to Carlyle, who said on receiving one of her yearly valentines, 'This comes from Mrs Cameron or the devil.' Sir Henry Taylor, a valued friend, says of her in his *Autobiography* (ii.18): 'If her husband was of a high intellectual order, and as such naturally fell to her lot, the friends that fell to her were not less so. Foremost of those all were Sir John Herschel and Lord Hardinge... Sir Edward Ryan, who had been the early friend of her husband, was not less devoted to her in the last days of his long life than he had been from the times in which they first met... It was indeed impossible that we should not grow fond of her – impossible for us, and not less so for the many whom her genial, ardent, and generous nature has captivated ever since.' A characteristic story of one of her many acts of persevering benevolence is told in the same volume (pp.185–8). Her influence on all classes was marked and admirable. She was unusually outspoken, but her genuine sympathy and goodness of heart saved her from ever alienating a friend.

At the age of fifty she took up photography, which in her hands became truly artistic, instead of possessing merely mechanical excellence. She gained gold, silver, and bronze medals in America, Germany, and England. She has left admirable portraits of many distinguished persons. Among her sitters were the Crown Prince and Princess of Prussia, Charles Darwin, Lord Tennyson, Mr. Browning, Herr Joachim, and Sir John Hershel, who had been her friend from her early girlhood. Mrs Cameron wrote many poems, some of which appeared in *Macmillan's Magazine*. Her only separate publication was a translation of Burger's *Leonora*, published in 1847.

[Personal Knowledge]   J. P. S.

3. Caroline Emilia Stephen.
Gift of Frederick R. Koch, The Harvard Theatre Collection, Houghton Library.

4. Anne Thackeray Ritchie.

5. Julia Margaret Cameron.

III
Friends

Virginia Woolf's memoirs of friends were written after those of her aunts, and are concerned more with the Bloomsbury Group than with her family life. Her views from the platform of time are now nearer. The obituary of Lady Strachey, materfamilias of the Stracheys, was written in 1928, and the memoir notes on her somewhat later. (Sadly Virginia wrote no memoir of her son Lytton, who died in 1932.) The private impressions and public talk on Roger Fry were done within a year after his death in 1934. The letter on Woolf's Greek teacher and friend Janet Case appeared the day Julian Bell's death was announced in 1937, and the tribute to Ottoline Morrell was written after her death the following year.

Jane Maria Strachey, born in 1840, was Bloomsbury's idea of what a Victorian matriarch could achieve. Energetic and literary, mother of a very large family, wife of General Sir Richard Strachey of the Raj, and herself a passionate imperialist yet also an ardent, formidable suffragist, Lady Strachey lived well into the later development of Bloomsbury, dying at the age of eighty-eight. Virginia Woolf wrote her tribute for the *Nation and Athenaeum*. It was signed only with her initials but readers of that journal – whose literary editor was Leonard Woolf – knew by 1928 the name the initials stood for. (Years before when Lytton Strachey asked if he could dedicate his *Queen Victoria* to 'V. W.', Virginia replied (25th January 1921), 'my inordinate vanity whispers might it not be Virginia Woolf in full? Some Victoria Worms or Vincent Woodlouse is certain to say it's them, and I want all the glory to be mine for ever.') In 1924 the *Nation and Athenaeum* had serialised excerpts from Lady Strachey's memoirs entitled 'Some Recollections of a Long Life'. The disjointed memoirs were a warning, Vanessa observed, for Virginia to begin her memoirs before she was eighty-five – as Virginia noted at the opening of 'Sketch of the Past'. Lady Strachey's recollections are, nevertheless, the basis for much of Virginia

Woolf's eulogy with its allusions to famous Anglo-Indian imperialists, the great actor Salvini, Robert Browning, George Eliot, etc. Virginia Woolf's account of the Strachey household drew on her and Leonard's memories of meals there, as well as on Lytton Strachey's Memoir Club paper about his Victorian-grotesque family home. When Lytton wrote to say Virginia's eulogy of his mother was perfect, she answered that she was relieved because she feared she had written only commonplaces, being unable to 'say the things that matter' (25th December 1928). To Lytton's sister Dorothy Bussy, who also praised the article, Virginia wrote that her sketch had been hurried, and although she had seen little of Lady Strachey she found her image 'predominating in my mind' (10th February 1929), which her memoir manages to convey.

When Lady Strachey's family gathered together some typed reminiscences entitled 'J.M.S.', Leonard Woolf wrote a brief recollection, and Virginia contributed five anecdotal notes from different times, four of which are set at various Strachey houses. The notes complement, in their personal tone, the formality of her *Nation and Athenaeum* tribute and have been used by her biographers, though never published completely until now. In both forms of recollection there remained constraints, of course, and nothing is said in them of Lady Strachey's disapproving attitudes, unprudish but still Victorian, toward indecency in literature or unconventional sexuality in her family.

The most extended memoir that Virginia Woolf wrote in the nineteenth-century sense of that term was her biography of Roger Fry, which she published the year before she died. Part of the biography was written alongside the 'Sketch of the Past' memoir notes that she thought of as a platform from which to regard past time. In her diary Virginia Woolf observed that the writing of *Roger Fry* had involved her in 'an odd posthumous friendship – in some ways more intimate than any I had in life' (30th December 1935).

That posthumous relationship began with two brief recollections of Fry that Woolf wrote before agreeing to do his biography. Like those of Lady Strachey, one was a public tribute, the other a series of personal impressions. Older than the other members of Bloomsbury, Fry too had been a Cambridge Apostle, but his impact on the group coincided with his first post-Impressionist exhibition of 1910 – an 'art-quake', in Desmond MacCarthy's term, that woke up England to modern art. At Fry's funeral in 1934, Virginia Woolf blamed herself once more for a lack of feeling that was connected again with Vanessa (see above, p. 11). His death was worse than Lytton Strachey's two years before, she noted in her diary: 'Such a blank wall! Such a silence. Such a poverty. How he reverberated. And I feel it through Nessa' (12th October 1934).

The impressions she noted down sometime later convey her detachment, but for more literary reasons. She mentions at the beginning the biographical experiment that Fry once planned, and in her diary (1st November 1934) she described another in which various friends were to contribute to a group biography of him. (Julian Bell and Anthony Blunt were to write on his later life, and Virginia and MacCarthy were to do Fry in Bloomsbury and then combine all the contributions.) Vanessa Bell was not listed among the potential contributors, although she wrote a Memoir Club paper shortly after Fry's death on which Virginia relied in her impressions. Woolf repeats in her notes that – using a term that had important feminist significance for her – she was an outsider when it came to art. In literature, of course, she was hardly that, and what she found so stimulating in Fry's criticism was his connecting post-Impressionism with fiction and poetry. Woolf's description of how he did this recapitulates what she had written years before in a Memoir Club paper on Old Bloomsbury, and which she would repeat again in her biography of Fry. Virginia Woolf also allows herself some of the freedom of fiction in her notes as she moves from remote figures in a Cambridge garden to the impressions, first of the nostalgic lecturer and painter of one cow, sheep or swan, and on to the contrasting Quixotic modernist artist who paints Jesus upside down and then applies post-Impressionism to interior decoration – a change Woolf conveys with her familiar symbolism of rooms. The impressions break off, the memoirist eventually becoming the 'more serious biographer' she hoped her sketch might serve.

At the start of her formal address opening a memorial exhibition of Roger Fry's paintings in Bristol on 12th July 1935, Virginia Woolf returns to her theme of the outsider. She was unaware that her audience, some of whom at least she assumed were familiar with Fry's books, would consist of '200 stout Burgesses' as she told Vanessa (14th July 1935). So instead of speaking about his paintings, Woolf says she wants to describe Roger Fry's talk. In doing so she mentions his Quaker integrity, something she was familiar with, through her Aunt Caroline. But to talk about Fry's talk involves her in crossing a central distinction of Fry's aesthetics, namely the separation of art and life. Woolf is nevertheless convinced that Fry's life reverberated in his criticism and his art. In describing this, she returns to one of her own crucial critical distinctions: the need for what she once called the granite of reason and the rainbow of sensibility. Virginia ends her address speculating on one more basic discrimination in Fry's career as well as her own: the interaction of the critical and the creative. Here Woolf has the delicate task of saying something not about Fry's great criticism but about the painting that he was so passionate about but which found him neither satisfaction nor success. In both her personal impressions and her public address, Virginia Woolf nevertheless shows how she could imagine as well as interpret in her post-humous friendship with Roger Fry.

The relationship of the memoir-writer and her subject recurs with the anonymous letter Virginia Woolf wrote to *The Times* on the death of her Greek teacher and feminist friend Janet Case. As was noted in the introduction to her memoir of Julian Bell, Woolf's tribute heads the obituary columns that include the notice of Julian Bell's death in Spain. Woolf's refusal to sign her letter was part of her 'new stand point' she said in Julian's memoir – a protest against the egomania of the times to which Julian belonged. To protect her creative unconscious she had developed in the 1930s what she labeled in her diary a 'philosophy of anonymity' (29th October 1933). It was a philosophy that fitted in well with her feminism. Later she described her biography of Roger Fry to the extroverted Ethel Smyth as 'an experiment in self suppression, a gamble on R's power to transmit himself' (16th August 1940). It would be interesting to look at the memoirs of Virginia Woolf collected here in the light of her self-expression or suppression. All the first-person pronouns in the Case obituary letter are Janet's. (Woolf's favorite pronoun, the only one she put in the title of a book, was *one*.)

The anonymity of the old pupil remembering her teacher fits, of course, with the admirable integrity of a reticent, contemplative woman able to be herself and still appreciate the egoism of such different young pupils as the shyly fierce Virginia Stephen or the socialite nymph Lady Diana Cooper. But Janet Case was also a feminist, active in the women's suffrage campaign and with the Women's Co-operative Guild of her Cambridge contemporary and friend Margaret Llewelyn Davies (for whom Virginia Woolf wrote the memoir also collected here). It was Margaret who asked Virginia to write about Janet in *The*

Times. Indeed it was Janet Case who initiated her pupil into the women's movement. Writing the letter for *The Times* on Janet was difficult, the result stiff and mannered, Woolf wrote in her diary, remembering how as a pupil she had loved Janet. Then she adds a remarkable comment about her teacher: 'how great a visionary part she played in my life, till the visionary became a part of the fictitious, not the real life' (19th July 1937). That fictive visionary life was not all to Janet Case's liking, however, as Virginia recorded over the years in her diary and letters. One criticism of Janet's mentioned in the diary particularly rankled – that the fiction of *Mrs Dalloway* was 'all dressing... technique' whereas the criticism of *The Common Reader*, also published in 1925, had 'substance' (13th September 1926). Apparently Janet Case did not consider *The Common Reader* essay 'On Not Knowing Greek' impertinent, as Virginia feared; it was in its own way an oblique tribute to Case's teaching.

The brief *Times* memoir of Janet Case provides an opportunity to return from the platform of the present to a past more than thirty years earlier. Preserved among the early journals of Virginia Stephen is a description of her Greek teacher when Janet was still Miss Case. 'Miss Case' is the only sketch devoted to one person in Virginia's 1903 diary. More self-conscious, less fluent than her obituary letter, the sketch nevertheless vividly conveys what learning Greek from Case meant for her young, humorous, 'contradictious' pupil whose grammar was rotten but whose literary understanding was finer – a legacy perhaps from her father's teaching, which put all grammar aside, she noted in her memoir of him, and went straight at the sense. It may have been Aeschylus rather than Euripides who described maidenhood so memorably, and there may be no instrumental genitive in Greek, yet clearly evident even in this early sketch is the modernist artist's disagreement with the moralising teacher. And how much more Virginia learned from Miss Case – the

Greek lessons continued with her after the sketch – than from Walter Pater's cultivated sister or the obscure Miss Clay. Janet Case's ability to argue firmly with her pupil yet see her point of view was part of the 'fine human sympathy' that Virginia says she had reason to test around the time her father was dying and later, as she recorded in a letter to Vanessa, when her half-brother George Duckworth was expressing unwanted affections for her (25th? July 1911).

Virginia Stephen also suggests in her 1903 diary an aspect of learning Greek from Miss Case that may illuminate her later comment on the part Janet played in her visionary life. A little before the sketch, Virginia recorded in her early diary a moment in which she saw

> how our minds are all threaded together – how any live mind today is of the very same stuff as Plato and Euripides. It is only a continuation & development of the same thing. It is this common mind that binds the whole world together & all the world is mind.

The Cambridge philosophy of Leonard Woolf and his friends would lead her to qualify this mentalism, but throughout her writings from this entry to works like *The Common Reader* and on to the mystical remarks in 'Sketch of the Past' and her last notes for the work she called *Anon*, Woolf expressed her fascination with the interrelations of past, present and future writers and readers.

Among the friends of Virginia Woolf's memoirs, there is a remarkable contrast between the reticent, contemplative Greek teacher and the flamboyantly aristocratic hostess for whom Woolf wrote obituary letters to *The Times* in 1937 and 1938. The contrast is manifested in the difference between the anonymity of an old pupil's letter on Janet Case and the opening words of the letter on Ottoline Morrell, where it is clearly announced that it is Virginia Woolf who is writing.

Two sketches from another recently discovered old diary of 1909 vividly display the dissimilarity of the two women. In the first Virginia Stephen recorded a visit to Hampstead and the Misses Case, Janet and her sister, together with their friend Margaret Llewelyn Davies; the ladies are a little shabby, austere, even stern, but together they remind Virginia of schoolgirls. From Hampstead Virginia Stephen goes in the next entry to 'A Modern Salon' of the great hostess Lady Ottoline Morrell in Bloomsbury. Virginia Woolf returned to her early diary sketch of Ottoline in the later Memoir Club paper on Old Bloomsbury. There she concluded that Ottoline would have to have a chapter, or at least an appendix to herself, in the Bloomsbury Group's history. (At one time or another she was intimately involved with both Roger Fry and Lytton Strachey.) 'Lustre and illusion' were the words Virginia Stephen used in her sketch, and which Virginia Woolf repeated in her paper to describe the salon of Ottoline whom Virginia would liken elsewhere to the Medusa or the Spanish Armada.

For all Lady Ottoline Morrell's hospitality to artists and others in London and later at the manor house of Garsington during the First World War (where conscientious objectors such as Clive Bell found refuge) she did not 'escape the ridicule of those whom she befriended', as Woolf notes in her obituary letter. The allusion is to the fictional caricatures of her by D.H. Lawrence, Aldous Huxley and others, but it could be extended to diaries and letters of Woolf herself. Ambivalence characterises both sides of Ottoline's and Virginia's thirty-year friendship. The young Virginia appeared at times to Ottoline in her journal as cold, cruelly observant, inhuman, while Virginia in her diary skewered Ottoline's egoism and 'slipperiness of soul' that then became part of the inspiration for the social world of *Mrs Dalloway* (4th June 1923). In the end, however, Lady Ottoline could incisively summarise Virginia Woolf as an enchanting, brilliant, ruthless, yet beloved friend. And Ottoline's death left Virginia feeling in her diary 'an intimacy abolished' (27th April 1938).

Virginia's final tribute to Ottoline's 'idealisms and exaltations' was again written, like Case's letter, at the urging of a friend – in this instance Ottoline's widower, Philip Morrell. In describing her as an artist whose inner freedom allowed her to create the world of a beautiful drawing room, Virginia Woolf paid Ottoline a supreme compliment and by means of a symbol that had such significance for Virginia herself.

The last words Virginia Woolf wrote about Lady Ottoline have the distinction of being the only work on which she collaborated with T.S. Eliot. In response to Philip Morrell's request for an epitaph, Virginia sent him the following, which she had composed with Eliot – and which Morrell rejected for his own Latin one:

Faithful and courageous
Most generous most gentle
In the weakness of her body
She preserved, nevertheless
A brave spirit, unbroken,
Delighting in beauty and goodness
And in the love of friends.

Lady Strachey: Obituary (1928)

There are some people who without being themselves famous seem to sum up the qualities of an age and to represent it at its best. Lady Strachey, who died last week at the age of eighty-eight, was among them. She seemed the type of the Victorian woman at her finest – many-sided, vigorous, adventurous, advanced. With her large and powerful frame, her strongly marked features, her manner that was so cordial, so humorous, and yet perhaps a little formidable, she seemed cast on a larger scale, made of more massive material than the women of today. One could not but be aware even to look at her that she was in the line of a great tradition. She came of a family famous for its administrators and public servants; she married into one of the great Anglo-Indian families of the nineteenth century. One could easily imagine how, had she been a man, she would have ruled a province or administered a Government department. She had all that instinct for affairs, that broad-minded grasp of politics that made the great public servant of the nineteenth century. But, in addition, like all Victorian women of her stamp, she was emphatically a mother and a wife. Even while she wrote dispatches at her husband's dictation and debated – for she was in the counsels of the men who governed India – this problem, that policy, she was bringing up, now in India, now in England, a family of ten children. She was presiding over one of those vast Victorian households which, chaotic as they seem now, had a character and a vitality about them which it is hard to suppose will ever be matched again. Memory provides a picture of the many-roomed house; of people coming and going; of argument; of laughter; of different voices speaking at once; of Lady Strachey herself a little absent-minded, a little erratic, but nevertheless the controller and inspirer of it all, now wandering through the rooms with a book, now teaching a group of young people the steps of the Highland reel, now plunging into ardent debate about politics or literature, now working out, with equal intentness, some puzzle in a penny paper which if solved would provide her with thirty shillings a week and a workman's cottage for life.

In her old age she wrote down a few memories of the past which show, very briefly, how naturally, how as a matter of course, she was in touch with the great figures of the Victorian world. She joked with Huxley; she exchanged spectacles with Tennyson; she was a special favourite with George Eliot, and, 'though much ashamed of my vanity in recording it', could not help remembering how 'Lewes told a friend of mine that I was his idea of Dorothea in *Middlemarch*.' She sat up to all hours of the night, 'eagerly discussing every aspect of humanity', with the most distinguished men of her time, openly but impersonally, rather as if they were in full evening dress, so it seems to a less formal age. For together with her keen interest in public questions, particularly in the education and emancipation of women, went an interest as vigorous in music and the drama, and especially in literature. She had a vast capacity for enthusiasm which fed happily and confidently as was common with the Victorians upon her own contemporaries and their works. She had no doubts whatever about the greatness of the men she knew and the lasting importance of their books. When she met Browning for the first time at a concert she wrote on her programme:

And did you once see Browning plain?
And did he stop and speak to you?

and kept it, a sacred relic. She counted it one of her great pieces of good luck that she was born contemporary with Salvini. She went to the theatre every night on which he acted. But she was not only attracted by the great figures of her own age. She was an omnivorous reader. She had her hands upon the whole body of English literature, from Shakespeare to Tennyson, with the large loose grasp that was so characteristic of the cultivated Victorian. She had a special love for the Elizabethan drama, and for English poetry – Beddoes was one of the obscure writers whom she championed and discovered – a little incongruously perhaps, for her own affinities seemed rather with the age of reason and the robust sense of the great English prose writers. She was, above all things, rational, positive, agnostic, like the distinguished men who were her friends. Later in life, after her husband's death, when her activities were somewhat lessened, though they were still varied enough to have filled the life of a younger woman, she would spend an entire winter's afternoon in reading an Elizabethan play from end to end. For reading aloud was one of her great natural gifts. She read with fire and ardour, and with a great clarity and distinction of utterance. Often she would pause to point out the beauty of some passage, or propound with extreme ingenuity some emendation, or impart a curious illustration that had stuck in her mind from her wide and miscellaneous foraging among books. Then, when the reading was over, she would launch out into stories of the past; of Lord Lytton and his sky-blue dressing gown; of Lord Roberts helping to mend her sewing machine; of Lawrence and Outram (she never passed the statue of Outram without making a salute, she said); of Pattles and Prinseps; of bygone beauties and scandals – for though she observed the conventions she was not in the least a prude; of Indian society fifty years, eighty years, a hundred years ago. For she had the Scottish love of following family histories and tracing the friendships and alliances of the present back to their roots in the past. Thus a haphazard party would come in her presence to have a patriarchal air, as she recalled the memories and the marriages that had bound parents and grandparents together years ago, in the distant past.

Gradually, though the vigour of her mind was as great as ever, it seemed to withdraw from modern life and to focus itself more and more upon the past. She did not remember clearly what had happened the week before, but Calcutta in 1870, Robert Browning's laugh, some saying of George Eliot's, were as clear, as dear, and as vivid as ever. It was her hard fate to lose her sight almost entirely some years before she died. She could no longer go foraging and triumphing through English litera-ture – for it seemed as if she carried on even the passive act of reading with something of the vigour with which she strode the streets, peering forward with her short-sighted eyes, or tossed her head high in a shout of laughter. But she could talk, she could argue, she could join in the disputes of the younger gener-ation and follow with pride the successes of her children. Her mind was still busy with literature, still active with suggestions for reviving forgotten plays, for editing old texts, for bringing to light some hidden splendour in those old books which she could no longer read herself, but almost commanded the younger generation to love as she had loved them. Her memory, grown to be the strongest part of her, still kept unimpaired in its depths some of the loveliest things in English poetry. When she was past eighty, she stopped one summer evening under a tree in a London square and recited the whole of 'Lycidas' without a fault. Last summer, though too weak to walk any more, she sat on her balcony and showered down upon the faces that she could not see a vast maternal benediction. It was as if the Victorian age in its ripeness, its width, with all its memories and achievements behind it were bestowing its blessing. And we should be blind indeed if we did not wave back to her a salute full of homage and affection.

J.M.S.: Notes (1929?)

Lancaster Gate – about 1903.
Pernel invited me to lunch there, but nobody paid me the least attention. Innumerable Stracheys were seated in silence round the dinner table. Sir Richard wrapt in a shawl sat in the middle. After a time James came in, laid a magazine in front of Sir Richard, who without saying anything produced a sixpenny bit and gave it him. Then Pippa said: 'What will you have, Papa? Cold beef or roast partridge?' 'Partridge' said Sir Richard. Lady Strachey threw up her hands. 'I *knew* he'd say that!' she exclaimed, 'So *I* must have cold beef!' That was the only thing that anybody said I think. All the same I thought it was a very amusing and exciting party.

About 1900.
The Stracheys had a house in the New Forest – my father took me to see them. Lady Strachey was in high glee. She had been routing about among the books and had discovered a first edition, I think of Ben Jonson. 'Look at that, Sir Leslie! Look at that!' she exclaimed, thrusting the book before him and pointing to an inscription on the title page – 'Ex dono Aùctoris'. My father looked and admired, but a little grimly I thought, and on the way home he said to me, 'I didn't like to tell Lady Strachey, but the accent should be on the second syllable of auctòris, not the first'.

Fitzroy Square – about 1908.
One summer afternoon I had dressed in complete evening dress for I was going to *The Ring* and was having tea alone when Lady Strachey was announced. She made no comment whatever either upon my evening dress or upon the fact which suddenly became obvious that our dog Hans had left a large brown

mound on the green carpet between us. She ignored both completely. I could not decide whether this was because she thought such things were unimportant or from good manners. After she had talked for about an hour with the greatest energy about Elizabethan poetry I decided that she had never seen either that I was in white satin or that Hans had misbehaved. She was thinking only of poetry. This impressed me greatly.

Belsize Park Gardens – during the war.
L.[Leonard] and I used to go to tea with her during the war. We always found her snipping up little bits of fancy paper with which she covered small cardboard boxes. 'My ideal life' she said once, 'would be to live *entirely* in boarding houses,' and she craned her long neck at me and fixed me with her eyes. 'I remember' she said 'seeing you as a child in an omnibus with your mother'. 'Which omnibus?' I asked, idiotically. 'How can I *possibly* tell you that?' she said scornfully. Yet I did not feel in the least snubbed, she was too majestic. And then, thinking of my mother, she launched out into a story about the Prinseps how some idiotic journalist had called Prinsep's Pier Princes Pier. 'They were grand men – kings of men, the Prinseps!' she exclaimed. Then she read us an Elizabethan play straight through. When she stopped, I asked if she liked any modern poetry. She shook her head in a melancholy way and pursed her lips. Then suddenly her face lit up. 'Yes! We've one living poet – one great living poet!' she exclaimed – 'Admiral Hopwood!' He had written a patriotic poem which she had cut out from *The Times* and read to us. That seemed odd, but all of a piece with her feeling for the Prinseps and the Indian Empire.

Gordon Square – late 2oties, I suppose.
One summer evening L. and I were walking past 51, and she was standing at the window with someone behind her. She was

then almost blind, but we waved up at her, and her maid must have told her who we were, for she strode at once out on to the balcony, leant over and flung her arms open as if she were embracing us – It was extraordinarily moving – very dramatic and yet perfectly simple. That was the last time I saw her.

6. Jane Maria Strachey.

A Series of Impressions (1934?)

In writing these impressions I have not aimed at accuracy of date or fact. I have tried to make a portrait of Roger Fry almost as a novelist might make a character in fiction. I have taken this course partly through inability to deal with his work from a critical point of view; and partly because he himself once offered to be the subject in a biographical experiment. He was to talk about himself, and I was to take notes and write a life in which fiction was to be allowed full play. Unhappily the sittings never took place. I have nothing but memory to depend upon; so that the portrait is merely an impressionist sketch written in the hope that it may serve a more serious biographer.

Many years ago two figures, a man and a woman, strolled in a garden on the banks of the Cam. Both were tall, there was a distinguished look about them. It was natural to ask, as they came by, Who are those people? 'Roger Fry and his wife' was the answer. It was a summer afternoon, and the two figures seemed for a moment to connect themselves with the beauty of the flowers and the willows and the sliding river. Next moment the picture had vanished.

The name Roger Fry however, insensibly gathered a certain meaning in the course of the next few years. In those quiet days before the war there was always somewhere in the background a little group of people who got up lectures, wished to revive ancient musical instruments, supported classical concerts, withstood the current taste in dress and furniture, and collected eighteenth century chairs and tables. Roger Fry – his name that is – seemed to be among them. When a circular, printed on hand made paper, announced a series of lectures on early Italian Art would be held at five thirty in Leighton House, it seemed fitting that Roger Fry should be the lecturer. His name suggested rows of people sitting soberly listening to some 'course' or other; and also it suggested very discreet water colour paintings, with one brown cow or one white sheep precisely in the right place; or an oil painting of a swan sailing on a lake, while a youth stretching over dabbles his hand in the placid waters. It seemed to be essential in those days if you cared for art, to dislike the present; to be perpetually occupied in trying to get back to a more austere and more peaceful age, when furniture was made by hand, an age when things were handmade, and dignified and rightly placed. Roger Fry was accepted by that world; and it seemed then that there was no reason why the two worlds of art lovers and philistines should not exist side by side, each going its own way and ignoring the other.

Those were the associations that made the name of Roger Fry dim and respectable.

Roger Fry's name had become rather dim and quiet.

Therefore it was a considerable surprise, some time about 1911, to meet Roger Fry for the second time in the flesh. There he was, the man who had walked in the garden that summer – the man who had spent the intervening years lecturing at Leighton House on Italian art. But in one second, in the time it took to open a door and come into a room, all those associations, all those preconceptions were torn up.

But...

Those three dots are a tribute to human weakness. When a whole conception is swept away and another substituted, the mind is so jumped out of its bearings that it is incapable of observation. Of course there must have been a gradual transition; he must have worn some tie, and have looked in this way or in that; but all these details have been obliterated, a series of impressions, chiefly of colour, had changed. By one single impression – the room is entirely different.

Strictly speaking in a material sense this was true. The chairs and tables were strewn with patterns of cotton made in Manchester for the natives of Africa. Propped up against the walls were pictures of chrysanthemum in pots which seemed to flare away like roaring fires of red paint. Then there was a still wet canvas, depicting Christ standing on his head; and a portrait of a lady whose left cheek was composed of a cheque upon which figures were still legible. Also there were several rough yellow white pots and hats worn by negresses made of black and white straw.

Where was the gentle Don who had lectured on Cimabue in Leighton House? He was nowhere. And what there was in his place was something so complex, so disturbing, so many sided, that it is tempting to poach on the novelists' preserves and to say that Roger Fry had been transformed into a Don Quixote; into a wildly fantastical knight, prancing across the prospect, hung with the queerest assortment of old tins and frying pans and chains – such as he looked once at a children's party, where he came dressed up at a cost of three and nine pence at Woolworths shop. There was something ridiculous laughable extravagant wildly amusing in the transformation that he made. Watts paintings vanished. Van Gogh took his place. Queen Anne chintz were over hung with African cottons. Superficially it was a source of constant shouts of laughter. It was like watching a pageant; standing in the street and cheering on the fantastic procession.

But no one was allowed to remain an outsider for long. For one thing, after the first shock and the amusement and the surprise and the laughter, his seriousness was apparent. And then again, the attack left art proper, and turned upon literature. It was then not so easy to stand outside and laugh. The method of his approach was by way of a little French book that had just appeared – Marie Claire by Marguerite Audoux. Soon that book was in everybodies' hands. 'D'you mean to tell me you've not read it? I've already given away twenty copies but here's another.' The book is now forgotten, but the discussions which it brought about still reverberate. For Marie Claire illustrated the fact that literature was affected by the same disease as painting. We writers were circling vaguely in the old eddies. We were using old cliches. We were using far too many adjectives. That was the line of the indictment. That led to frequent recourse to the book-case. Dante was the supreme poet, not Shakespeare. Wordsworth was the greatest of the moderns. Shelley was convicted. Keats was suspected. And he set to work with a pencil upon modern poets and novelists; underlined their useless adjectives, their merely literary phrases. All that was 'dim', romantic, all that echoed and reverberated was abhorent.

Memorial Exhibition Address (1935)

When I was asked to open this exhibition of Roger Fry's pictures my first instinct I admit was to refuse, for it seemed to me that an exhibition of paintings ought to be opened by a painter or by a critic of painting. But on second thoughts it struck me that this particular exhibition, this memorial exhibition of Roger Fry's pictures, might fitly be opened by someone who is not a painter or a critic because Roger Fry did more than anyone to make such people – such outsiders – enjoy looking at pictures. That was my experience, and I think I am right in saying that there are others in this room who have felt the same thing. Pictures were to many of us – if I may generalise – things that hung upon walls; silent inscrutable patterns; treasure houses with locked doors in front of which learned people would stop, and about which they would lecture, saying that they were of this period or of that, of this school or of that, probably by this master, but perhaps on the other hand by one of his disciples. And we would trail behind them, silent, servile, and bored. Then all of a sudden those dim pictures began to flash with light and colour; and our guides, those respectable professors, began to argue and to quarrel, called each other – if I remember rightly – liars and cheats, and altogether began to behave like living people arguing about something of vital importance. What had happened? What had brought this life and colour, this racket and din into the quiet galleries of ancient art? It was that Roger Fry had gathered together the Post-Impressionist Exhibition in Dover Street; and the names of Cézanne and Gauguin, of Matisse and Picasso, suddenly became as hotly debated, as violently defended as the names – shall we say? – of Ramsay MacDonald, Hitler, or Lloyd George. That is many years ago. The dust of that conflict has died down. But all the same pictures have never gone back to their walls. They are no longer silent, decorous, and dull. They are things we live with, and laugh at, love and discuss. And I think I am right in saying that it was Roger Fry more than anybody who brought about this change. He did it, of course, by his writing and by his lecturing. Many of you will have read his books, and will have heard his lectures. You will know better than I can describe it how profoundly he felt about the roots of art; how subtly, with that long white wand of his, standing in front of his magic lantern, he would point to this line and to that and would bring to the surface in new and startling revelation those qualities that lie deep sunk in pictures so that we saw them afresh. You will have felt this while he lectured; you will still find it, happily, in his books; but I would like, if I can, to give you some faint idea how he did it in his talk.

I remember an instance that struck me greatly one night last summer. It was at a friend's house, and someone had brought him a picture for his opinion. It was a question whether it was a genuine picture by Degas, or whether it was an extremely skilful imitation. The picture was stood on a chair, and Roger Fry sat and looked at it. His eye ranged over it, carefully, appreciatively. It was a very good picture beyond a doubt; it was signed by Degas; it was in the manner of Degas – he was inclined to think on the whole that it was by Degas. And yet there was something that puzzled him; something – he could not say what – that made him hesitate. As if to rest himself he turned away and took part in a discussion that was going forward in another corner of the room – a difficult discussion upon some abstract question of aesthetics. He argued and he listened to others arguing. But now and again I saw his eye go back to the picture as if it were feeling it, tasting it, making a voyage of discovery on its own. Then there was a pause. Suddenly he looked up and said: 'No. No. That is not by Degas.'

There it seemed to me one had a glimpse for a moment into the process that made him so great a critic. While he was arguing about the theory of art in the abstract his eye was ranging over the picture and bringing back its spoils. Then there was a moment of fusion, of comprehension; and his mind was made up. 'No,' he said. 'It is not by Degas.' But how was it done? By the union, it seemed to me, of two different qualities – his reason and his sensibility. Many people have one; many people have the other. But few have both, and fewer still are able to make them both work in harmony. But that was what he did. While he was reasoning he was seeing; and while he was seeing he was reasoning. He was acutely sensitive, but at the same time he was uncompromisingly honest. Was this integrity, this honesty, a quality that he owed in part to his Quaker blood? He came, as you know, of a great Quaker family, and I have sometimes thought that this clarity, this sobriety of judgment, this determination to get beneath the appearance to the bedrock beneath are qualities that go with a Quaker up-bringing. At any rate he never allowed himself merely to feel; he always checked and verified his impressions. Whether he upset other people's views (as he did) or changed his own (and he did), he always used his brain to correct his sensibility. And what was of equal importance, he always allowed his sensibility to correct his brain.

Here I come to a point in speaking of him where I doubt if he would let me go on. For I want to say that his understanding of art owed much to his understanding of life, and yet I know that he disliked the mingling and mixing of different things. He wanted art to be art; literature to be literature; and life to be life. He was an undaunted enemy of the sloppiness, the vague-ness, the sentimentality which has filled so many academies with anecdotes of dogs and duchesses. He detested the story-telling spirit which has clouded our painting and confused our criticism. But I will venture to say that one of the reasons why his criticism always grew, always went deeper, always included more, and never froze into the rigidity of death was that he himself breasted so many different currents of the stream of life. He was a man of many interests and many sympathies. As a young man he had been trained as a scientist. Science interested him profoundly. Poetry was one of his perpetual delights. He was deeply versed in French literature. He was a great lover of music. Anything that he could touch and handle and fashion with his fingers fascinated him. He made plates and pots with his own hands; he dyed stuffs; he designed furniture; he would come into the kitchen and teach the cook how to make an omelette; he would come into the drawing-room and teach the mistress how to arrange a bunch of flowers. And just as connoisseurs would bring him a picture for his opinion, so people of all kinds – and he had friends of all kinds – would bring him their lives – those canvases upon which we paint so many queer designs – and he would bring to bear upon their muddles and misfortunes the same rare mixture of logic and sympathy that made him so invigorating as a critic. He would start people living again just as he would start them painting again. And though I do not want to mix up different things, still I believe it was because so many interests, so many sympathies lived together in him that his teaching remained so fertile and so fresh.

But there was another reason why his criticism never became, as criticism so often does become, the repetition of a fixed idea. And that was of course that he always painted himself. He cared more for his painting than for his writing. The writing was done with many groans in the afternoon when the light was bad; on the tops of omnibuses; in the corners of third-class railway carriages. But painting was an instinct – a delight. If one were walking with him through the English fields, or driving with him along the roads of Italy or Greece, suddenly he would stop, and look. 'I must just make a note of that,' he would say, and out would come a pencil and a piece of paper and he would make a rough-and-ready sketch on the spot.

Many of the pictures on these walls are the results of those sketches. And because he painted himself he was perpetually forced to meet with his own brush those problems with which he was dealing with his pen. He knew from his own experience what labours, joys, despairs, go to the making of pictures. A picture was to him not merely the finished canvas but the canvas in the making. Every step of that struggle, which ends sometimes in victory, but more often in defeat, was known to him from his own daily battle. It was because he painted himself that he kept so keen a sense of all the intricate processes of painting; and that was why he had so high a standard of what I may call the morality of art. No one knew better than he did how hard it is to paint well; no one knew better than he did how easy it is to palm off upon the public something that does instead. That is why his criticism is so trenchant, so witty, often so devastating in its exposure of humbug and pretence. That too is why it is so full of respect and admiration for the artist who has used his gift honourably and honestly even though it is a small one.

He was never, I think, satisfied with his own painting; he never met with the success which he deserved. But that made no difference to his interest, to his activity. He went on painting; he went on tearing up his pictures; he threw them away; he began them again. And his devotion to his art seemed, if possible, to grow stronger with the years. Had he lived to be a hundred he would have been found, I am sure, sitting in front of a canvas with a brush in his hand.

Therefore there is nothing that he would have liked more than that you should have brought together this collection of his paintings. And there is no exhibition that could rouse questions of greater interest. We may ask ourselves, as we look at these pictures, is it a good thing that an artist should be also a critic, or does it inhibit his creative power? Is it necessary that an artist, in order to use his genius fully, should live half submerged in the dim world of ignorance, or on the contrary does know-ledge and the consciousness that comes with it lead him to be more daring and more drastic in his researches and discoveries, and so prolong his artistic life and give it new power and direc-tion? Such questions can be answered here as in no other room in England; for no artist, I think I am right in saying, knew more about the problems of his art than Roger Fry, or pursued them with a deeper curiosity or with greater courage.

But here I touch upon questions that lie beyond my scope – here I come to the pictures themselves; and I am not able to speak of Roger Fry's pictures as a fellow painter or as a fellow critic would speak of them. But speaking unprofessionally, as an outsider, I am sure that Roger Fry, were he here, would have made us all welcome equally to his exhibition. He would have asked only that we should come to it, whatever our calling, whatever our interests, with open eyes and open minds in the spirit of enjoyment. He believed that the love of art lives in most people if they will but give scope to it. He believed that the understanding of art, the enjoyment of art, are among the most profound and enduring pleasures that life has to give. I feel then that I am now asking you to embark upon a voyage – upon a voyage in which he will always be one of the great leaders, the great captains – a voyage of discovery into the mind and art of a remarkable man; and I have great pleasure in declaring this exhibition open.

Recollections (1937)

An Old Pupil's Recollections
MISS JANET CASE
CLASSICAL SCHOLAR AND TEACHER

An old pupil writes:

The death of Janet Case last Thursday will bring back to many of her old pupils the memory of a rare teacher and of a remarkable woman. She was a classical scholar, educated at Girton, and there must still be some Cambridge men who remember her, a noble Athena, breaking down the tradition that only men acted in the Greek play. When she left Cambridge she settled in London and for many years earned her living by teaching in schools and in private houses a great variety of pupils, some seriously to pass examinations, others less seriously to read Greek for their own amusement.

Undoubtedly if the pupil were in earnest Janet Case was a highly competent tutor. She was no dilettante: she could edit a Greek play and win praise from the great Verrall himself. But if the pupil were destined to remain an amateur Janet Case accepted the fact without concealing the drawbacks and made the best of it. The grammar was shut and the play opened. Somehow the masterpieces of Greek drama were stormed, without grammar, without accents, but somehow, under her compulsion, so sane and yet so stimulating, out they shone, if inaccessible still supremely desirable. And then the play was shut, and with her generous tolerance for youth and its egoism she would let herself be drawn into argument, made to discuss modern fiction, since she had said that Euripides reminded her of Meredith; made to thrash out the old problem of artist and teacher, since she had said that Aeschylus reminded her of Wordsworth. And so by transitions, rising naturally from the play, last night's party was reached, and the frock that was worn and the talk that was talked at last night's party, until even she could stretch her one hour no farther but must cycle off, with her little bag of text books, to teach another pupil, perhaps in Islington, perhaps in Mayfair.

In a pencilled note written a few days before her death she recalled how Lady D. 'used to come to her lesson like a nymph scarcely dry from her bath in a gauze wrap... and used to say "My good woman" in an expostulatory tone when I objected to an adjective not agreeing with its noun or some such trifle.' The words, with their humorous appreciation both of the nymph and of the noun, serve to explain why it was that she who was both so sound a scholar and so fine and dignified a presence, never held any of those posts that might have given her an academic position and saved her from the stress of private teaching. She enjoyed too many things – teaching a real scholar, and teaching a real worldling, going in and out of pupils' houses, noting their characters, divining their difficulties – she enjoyed them all too much and music and acting and pictures to concentrate upon one ambition.

The little house in Hampstead where her sister taught children, and friends came, and old pupils brought her new problems to solve, made a happier setting for her buoyant and unfettered spirit than any college. Her Greek was connected with many things. It was connected, naturally, seeing that she was the niece of Sir James Stansfeld, the reformer, with the life, with the politics of her day. She found time for committees, for the suffrage, for the Women's Co-operative Guild, of which her friend Margaret Llewelyn Davies was secretary; for all causes that were then advanced and in dispute. In her way she was a pioneer; but her way was one that kept her in the background, a counsellor rather than a champion, listening to the theories of others with a little chuckle of merriment, opening her beautiful veiled eyes with a sudden flash of sympathy and laughter, but for herself she wanted no prominence, no publicity. She was contemplative, reticent, withdrawn.

In the last years, after her health had broken down, she 'retired': but the word only signified that she had again extended her scope, this time most happily to enjoy with her sister what London had denied her – a country garden, the grass rides and ancient avenues of the New Forest. What have I done, she once asked, standing under a beech tree, to deserve all this? And echo might have answered: 'You have been yourself.' In the Forest she lived very quietly: she gave up teaching. When an old pupil reproached her, for were there no other girls to whom Janet Case could teach Greek without grammar? she said that the country left her no time. There was always something to do: a bird to watch; a flower to plant; her sister to talk to; and the Forest itself – how could one bear to leave it unseen? But that lesson she had learnt, and to sit by her side when she knew that death was near was to be taught once more a last lesson, in gaiety, courage, and love.

Miss Case (1903)

Two days ago I had my Greek lesson from Miss Case. I reflect that it may be my last, after a year & a half's learning from her – so wish, entirely presumptuously I know, to make a rough sketch, which is at any rate done from life.

When I first saw her one afternoon in the drawing room, she seemed to me exactly what I had expected – tall, classical looking, masterfull. But I was bored at being taught, & for some time, only did just what was asked from me, & hardly looked up from my book – that is at my teacher. But she was worth looking at. She had fine bright eyes – a curved nose, the teeth too prominent indeed but her whole aspect was vigorous & wholesome. She taught well too. My varied experience of Greek teachers makes me a good judge of their merits I think. She was more professional than Miss Pater though perhaps not so cultivated – she was more genial than Miss Clay & as good a scholar. But I am sorry to say – really now a little repentant – that she did not at first attract me. She was too cheerful & muscular. She made me feel 'contradictious' as the nurses used to say. After a time I found out her line of teaching, & rather set my back against it – at least I discovered certain opinions which she held very vigorously – & which when contradicted, were worth a good half hours discussion. I contradicted them; advanced life long opinions on the spur of the moment, & to my delight she took me quite seriously – or when I was in a lazy mood, drew her out; gave in at this point, led her on to another – & when she was fairly started on some theory of hers – let my mind stray. I began this system in pure idleness; it relieved the tedium of Greek grammar & continued it from a genuine interest with a little malice mixed – I found out that she had theories of her own about the Furies; for six lessons I too had theories about the Furies: – & so with many other subjects. She was a person of ardent theories & she could expound them fluently. She used three adjectives where I could only lay hands on one – Aeschylus was strenuous, grand, impassioned & so on. But she was no sentimentalist: she had her grammar at her finger tips – she used to pull me up ruthlessly in the middle of some beautiful passage with 'Mark the *ar*'. I read a very lovely description of maidenhood in Euripides (?) for instance – how the maiden hangs like ripened fruit within the orchard – but the gates ajar, the passer by spies in – & does not hesitate to pluck. That was the sense of it, & at the end I paused with some literary delight in its beauty. Not so Miss Case. 'The use of the instrumental genitive in the 3rd line is extremely rare' her comment upon Love! But that is not a fair example; & at any rate I think it really praiseworthy; aesthetic pleasure is so much easier to attain than knowledge of his uses of the genitive – I think it is true that she read with a less purely literary interest in the text than I did; she was not by any means blind to the beauties of Aeschylus and Euripides (her two favourite writers) but she was not happy till she had woven some kind of moral into their plays.

She was always expounding their 'teaching' and their views upon life & Fate, as they can be interpreted by an intelligent reader. I had never attempted anything of this kind before, & though I protested that Miss Case carried it too far, yet I was forced to think more than I had done hitherto – & interested accordingly. It was upon these subjects that she became really eloquent. She would spend a whole lesson in defining the relation of Aeschylus towards Fate – or the religious peculiarities of Euripides. This was the side of the thing that most interested her – & to her great credit, she made me, at least, see her point of view. Then there was our grammar. Many teachers have tried to break me in to that – but with only a passing success. Miss Case went to the root of the evil; she saw that my foundations were rotten – procured a Grammar, & bade me start with the very first exercise – upon the proper use of the article – which I had hitherto used with the greatest impropriety. She never failed to point out, with perfect good humour that my exercises were detestable – 'I haven't even attempted to correct this one' she said once – with the cheerful laugh, which spoke of an undaunted courage. I never once made her lose her temper, though I sometimes lost mine sufficiently to wish I could. Now that our lessons are over – for good perhaps – I am amazed at the amount she stood from me –

But in all these ways she was an excellent teacher. I feel besides, that she is a really valiant strong minded woman, in a private capacity. We strayed enough from grammar to let me see this. She talked on many subjects, & on all she showed herself possessed of clear strong views, & more than this she had the rare gift of seeing the other side; she had too, I think, a fine human sympathy which I had reason once or twice to test –

This, I know is most inadequate testimony to her – but under the circumstances of haste & discomfort, I can do no better.

I vaguely hope too, that our parting is not yet really final –

Obituary Letter (1938)

Virginia Woolf writes:—

The remarkable qualities of Ottoline Morrell – her originality, her courage, the personal ascendancy that created so memorable a society – have already been noted in your columns. Still the desire remains to testify, however imperfectly, to the splendid use she made of those rare gifts of fortune and of character. The great lady who suddenly appeared in the world of artists and writers immediately before the War easily lent herself to caricature. It was impossible not to exclaim in amazement at the strangeness; at the pearls, at the brocades, at the idealisms and exaltations. Again, with what imperious directness, like that of an artist intolerant of the conventional and the humdrum, she singled out the people she admired for qualities that she was often the first to detect and champion, and brought together at Bedford Square and then at Garsington, Prime Ministers and painters, Bishops and freethinkers, the famous and the obscure! Whether she sat at the head of her table against a background of pale yellow and pomegranate, or mused at Garsington with her embroidery on her lap and undergraduates at her feet, or held on her way down the Tottenham Court Road like a Renaissance princess listening to inaudible music while the passers by stared, she created her own world. And it was a world in which conflicts and collisions were inevitable; nor did she escape the ridicule of those whom she befriended.

But beneath this exotic appearance, sometimes so odious to her – 'Look at my hands!' she once protested. 'How ugly they are!' – there was a complex nature. She boasted, whether fancifully or not, of a French washerwoman among her ancestresses. Certainly there was a raciness in her refinement; a democratic spirit which led her not only to flout the conventions of the world, but to keep her house bravely open during the War to the unpopular and the friendless. It was that inner freedom, that artist's vision, that led her past the decorated drawing-room with all its trappings to the actual workshop where the painter had his canvas, and the writer his manuscript. The 'great hostess' was very humble in the presence of those who could create beauty; and very generous; and very sincere. For beneath the glamour which she created as inevitably as the lily pours out scent, there was a diffident and shrinking spirit. As the years passed this became more and more apparent. Deafness had grown upon her and she was often ill. She accepted such trials with aristocratic, or, it may be, with devout composure. She made no more efforts to gather the many coloured reins into her own hands; to drive her team with reckless courage through a world that, she felt, was destroying all she cherished. Rather she was content to sit back in the corner of her sofa working at her embroidery still, but no longer presiding. There in the evening, alone, even lovelier in her black than in her brocade, she would talk of the people she had known; of some new poem she had liked; of some unknown poet she had met; and of London, whose beauty she loved; and of that English country that was so dear to her – the country round Welbeck; and of the eccentricities of her forebears; of the old Duke who dug the tunnels; and how she had run through the great rooms as a child discovering pictures; and of the ardours and failures of her life; and of Shelley and Keats – until at last, at last, it was time to go from the room which she had made so beautiful.

7. From left to right, Janet Case, Virginia Stephen, Vanessa Bell.
Gift of Frederick R. Koch, The Harvard Theatre Collection, Houghton Library.

8. Ottoline Morrell.

IV
Occasions

Two of Virginia Woolf's uncollected memoirs are memories of groups rather than individuals. One unfortunately is just a fragment on hoaxing the Royal Navy, but the other is the longest explicitly autobiographical piece that she published and a remarkable statement of her class consciousness and her feminism.

In June 1913, less than a year after they married, Virginia and Leonard Woolf were invited by the general secretary of the Women's Co-operative Guild – the largest and most significant working women's organisation in England – to attend their Congress at Newcastle-on-Tyne. The general secretary was Janet Case's old friend Margaret Llewelyn Davies. Virginia had introduced Margaret to Leonard, who then became deeply interested in co-operative socialism, writing several books on the subject. The Woolfs thoroughly enjoyed the Congress, Leonard wrote afterwards, thanking Margaret. Virginia added a note: 'Being ignorant doesnt mean that one cant at least appreciate (however, being ignorant only applies to me) V. W.' (13th June 1913).

Seventeen years later Virginia Woolf described the memory of the Congress. Appreciation and enjoyment were not exactly what she remembered. Ignorance certainly was, and irritation and depression, as she looked back from the temporal platform of May 1930 to the political platform of the Congress. The occasion for her published memoir was an introductory letter to a collection of memoirs and letters by the married working women of the Co-operative Guild, edited by Margaret Llewelyn Davies. In 1915 Margaret had edited the very successful *Maternity: Letters from Working-Women Collected by the Women's Co-operative Guild*. Virginia told Margaret she found the letters 'so amazing', but the Woolfs were just starting their Hogarth Press and could not publish it (22nd February 1915). By 1929, Leonard and Virginia Woolf were keen to have their

Hogarth Press publish this new collection. Margaret exacted a reluctant 'Introductory Letter' from Virginia, who felt that she was 'too much of a picturesque amateur' to do it (6th June 1929). The book was called *Life as We Have Known It*, its authors being described as Co-operative Working Women; photographs of the Congresses and the memoir-writers were also included. The paradoxical theme of the introduction, however, was that life as these women had known it was not life as Virginia Woolf had known it.

Two memories are the focus of Woolf's introductory letter: the experience of the Congress and a visit later that summer to the Guild's London headquarters. In describing the visit, Woolf said she was telescoping many discussions with the formidable Margaret – described elsewhere in a letter of Virginia's as a woman who 'could compel a steam roller to waltz' (28th May 1913). Virginia Woolf is troubled in her memories of both the Congress and the discussions with Margaret by what she feels is her fictitious, aesthetic sympathy with working women. At the Congress Virginia's attempts at imagining the lives of the women become too much a game. The barrier seems impassable between working women and capitalist ladies (among whom were Margaret herself and her friend and assistant Lilian Harris, but not the clerk Miss Kidd). Eventually wealth will be shared, Virginia wrote, all life will become richer, but only after they are all dead. ('The long run' is an inadequate guide to current affairs, John Maynard Keynes said famously in 1923, because 'in the long run we are all dead'.)

The chasm of class is spanned in Woolf's memoir not by altruistic compassion or games of let's pretend, but by the imaginative value for the reader that inheres in the memoirs and letters of working women, to which can be added the imaginative value that comes from Virginia Woolf's own description of these women. The form of Woolf's memoir is complex. It is framed as a letter to Margaret Llewelyn Davies but the letter-writer's point of view shifts back and forth between the singular and the plural – between what 'we' felt and 'I' felt. The 'we' is not explicitly identified, and does not need to be, given the name of the author, the co-operative writings of her husband, their friendship with Davies and the joint ownership of the press (announced as always on the title page) that published the memoirs and letters Virginia was introducing. But her letter is also a memoir about memoirs – those of the working women that she is introducing. Their memoirs illuminate hers of the Congress, and her conclusion is not simply aesthetic: 'since writing is a complex art [she wrote 'impure art' in the first version], much infected by life, these pages have some qualities even as literature that the literate and the instructed might envy.'

Virginia Woolf nevertheless agreed with Davies in a letter after reading the proofs of her introduction that she made too much of the literary side of her interest, and not enough of the humane (1st February 1931). She is intrigued, for example, at the Guild's headquarters by the symbolic colours of the three women: Davies is kingfisher blue, Harris's dress is coffee-coloured, and Miss Kidd wears a deep shade of purple. Writing the letter had been difficult for Woolf; it took two or even three weeks of hard work and she resolved in her diary never again 'to use one's art as an act of friendship' (6th July 1930). But that was not all. Some of the co-operative women wanted changes – 'intolerable hedgings', Virginia called them in a letter, which she somehow had to circumvent (28th August 1930).

Virginia Woolf actually wrote two different versions of her letter. The first was for an American periodical; it disguised the location of the Congress and the names of Davies, Harris and Kidd, and was given the title 'Memories of a Working Women's Guild'. The revised version (separately printed here for the first time) used real names and made some of the requested changes (the pipe-smoking, detective-story-reading Lilian Harris is deprived of her pipe and her stories). There are also substantive alterations and additions, most strikingly in the comments on the working women's criticism of ladies. Added, for instance, was Virginia Woolf's definition of what ladies desire – 'things that are ends, not things that are means'; and altered was the criticism of working women's deriding ladies' knowledge of reality, now described as 'foolish' rather than 'bad manners'.

The experience of writing her introductory letter, Virginia told Margaret, left her with an appalled sense of 'the terrific conventionality of the workers' whom she thought had taken on 'all the middle-class respectabilities which we – at any rate if we are any good at writing or painting – have faced and thrown out' (10th October 1930).

Afterwards, however, Virginia Woolf was relieved at the appreciative response to her introduction from guild women that Davies sent her, though she still felt someone else than a writer should have done the introduction. But that did not keep her from wondering a few years later if perhaps they might do another book together. They did not, but Woolf's memoir and commentary on working women's memoirs, with its echoes of *A Room of One's Own* (1929) and anticipations of *Three Guineas* (1938), remains one of her most enlightening autobiographical essays.

Ten years after describing her memories of the Women's Co-operative Guild, Virginia Woolf returned in her memoirs to 1910 and the occasion of the celebrated *Dreadnought* Hoax in which she participated with her brother Adrian, Duncan Grant and some other of Adrian's friends. In a talk she called her *Dreadnought* notes in her diary (2nd September 1940), Virginia retold the story to the Rodmell Women's Institute and then The Memoir Club, leaving her audience 'helpless with laughter', according to E.M. Forster. Only the last few pages of what appears to have been a twenty-four-page talk have survived, and they were taken in part from Adrian Stephen's *The Dreadnought Hoax* that the Hogarth Press had published four years earlier. (Adrian, a psychiatrist, cites his qualification as a truth-teller to recount the hoax, insisting that as he is not a literary person, he had not the imagination to tell falsehoods.) In the aftermath of the famous hoax, which included newspaper stories and questions in parliament, Virginia Stephen allowed herself to be interviewed as 'the Lady Prince' of the hoax by the *Daily Mirror* – the only interview she is known to have given, and one that allows a return from the platform of 1940 to the past time of 1910.

The lost parts of Woolf's *Dreadnought* memoir presumably recounted how Adrian Stephen and some college friends, organised by Horace de Vere Cole, disguised themselves as the Sultan of Zanzibar's uncle and his suite and hoaxed the mayor of Cambridge. Cole then conceived the idea of hoaxing the navy, aided and abetted by Adrian, who wanted to pull the leg of his first cousin, William Fisher (whose name he concealed in his account), the flag commander of Britain's largest battleship at the time. According to Quentin Bell, who heard Virginia's talk at The Memoir Club, her involvement was almost accidental; in the absence of friends who were to take part, Virginia was asked two days before to join what was to be the Emperor of Abyssinia's suite. Why Abyssinia? England maintained cordial relations with Ethiopia, to use the country's modern name, but perhaps there was a vestigial literary influence of Samuel Johnson's familiar *Rasselas: Prince of Abyssinia*.

Virginia, Adrian and Duncan were joined by Cole and two other friends. Cole represented the Foreign Office in a top hat, Adrian in a bowler and fake beard was to be the interpreter and the others, in blackface, false lips and beards, were robed by a costumer to resemble Abyssinians. A forged tele-gram was sent from the Foreign Office to the *Dreadnought* announcing a Prince Makelen of Abyssinia (not the Emperor as Adrian has it) and his suite were to visit the ship. The hoaxers took the train to Weymouth, were carried to the ship by the admiral's launch, and proceeded to tour the ship, with Adrian translating in garbled Latin and the others responding with words such as 'bunga bunga' or Virginia's 'chuck-a-choi, chuck-a-choi', according to some accounts. Amazingly, the hoax worked. The group returned to London by train (after making railway officials buy gloves to serve the meals); a commemorative photograph was taken and they dispersed. Horace Cole leaked the story to the Foreign Office and the newspapers. Later, boys in the streets taunted sailors and musical comedians improvised on the words 'bunga bunga' (with its echoes of bungle and bugger).

The repercussions for the navy, the Admiralty and the hoaxers are partly described in Virginia's notes and inter-view. What she brings out is the degree to which the hoax was a family matter for her and Adrian. William Fisher's older brother, the influential don Herbert, wrote Virginia an irate letter, she remembered in a letter more than twenty years later, about '"vulgar playing tricks on the King's ships – for God's sake keep your name out of it" – damn my name – his name he meant...' (6th October 1932). William Fisher told Adrian the navy mess was calling her a prostitute, and cousin Dorothea Stephen wrote saying the hoax showed just how much Virginia needed religion. Vanessa Bell was appalled at the physical risks Virginia had taken, and her husband Clive was as angry as the Fishers and the Stephen cousin at her involvement in the escapade. When Admiral Sir William Fisher died in 1937, Virginia wrote in a letter that her last meeting with him had been 'on the deck of the *Dreadnought* in 1910, I think; but

I wore a beard. And I'm afraid he took it to heart a good deal – so I've heard' (28th June 1937).

The honorary beatings and family connection that Virginia describes in her notes were satirised by Woolf herself in a 1920 story she called 'A Society'. (The title is a take-off of the Apostles, who called themselves The Society.) The story describes a group of women who form a society for asking questions; one of them was to visit a man-of-war and her report tells

> how she had dressed herself as an Aethiopian Prince and gone aboard one of His Majesty's ships. Discovering the hoax, the Captain visited her (now disguised as a private gentleman) and demanded that honour should be satisfied.

Honour is satisfied with six ceremonial cane taps on the behind. Then the disguised gentleman demands that her/his honour must be satisfied, which it is with four and a half strokes in the small of the Captain's back, after he is terribly shocked at the hoaxer's proposing to establish class credentials by mentioning his/her mother's name. As 'A Society' shows, Virginia's almost fortuitous involvement in the *Dreadnought* Hoax added a significant feminist aspect to it, extending its ridicule from the navy to the patriarchy. It was not simple coincidence that a month before the hoax Janet Case had involved Virginia in working for the women's suffrage movement.

Looking back at the *Dreadnought* Hoax as its centenary approaches, it is difficult not to be struck with what Quentin Bell has called 'the lunatic audacity' of the pre-war hoaxers – dreadnoughts themselves, certainly – and at the stolid obtuseness of the navy. One friend remembered Woolf retelling the story to show how naval hearts of oak were accompanied by heads of the same substance. A family joke, but also very much an anti-establishment class joke and finally an anti-imperialist one in which upper-middle-class costumed, black-faced gentlemen and a lady speaking gibberish could uncover the preposterous ignorance of the officers and sailors of the home fleet's flagship, with their antique codes of martial honour. An ironic afterthought on the affair was a penned insertion by Virginia Woolf in her typed notes. Observing that rules and regulations were changed following the hoax so that it would no longer be possible to repeat it, she added 'I am glad to think that I too have been of help to my country.'

A final page of Woolf's talk refers to a visit of the real Emperor of Abyssinia soon after the hoax. In fact, the emperor, Menelik II, was incapacitated by strokes in 1910 and could not have visited England.

Life as We Have Known It (1931)

When you asked me to write a preface to a book which you had collected of papers by working women I replied that I would be drowned rather than write a preface to any book whatsoever. Books should stand on their own feet, my argument was (and I think it is a sound one). If they need shoring up by a preface here, an introduction there, they have no more right to exist than a table that needs a wad of paper under one leg in order to stand steady. But you left me the papers, and, turning them over, I saw that on this occasion the argument did not apply; this book is not a book. Turning the pages, I began to ask myself what is this book then, if it is not a book? What quality has it? What ideas does it suggest? What old arguments and memories does it rouse in me? And as all this had nothing to do with an introduction or a preface, but brought you to mind and certain pictures from the past, I stretched my hand for a sheet of notepaper and wrote the following letter addressed not to the public but to you.

You have forgotten (I wrote) a hot June morning in Newcastle in the year 1913, or at least you will not remember what I remember, because you were otherwise engaged. Your attention was entirely absorbed by a green table, several sheets of paper, and a bell. Moreover you were frequently interrupted. There was a woman wearing something like a Lord Mayor's chain round her shoulders; she took her seat perhaps at your right; there were other women without ornament save fountain pens and despatch boxes – they sat perhaps at your left. Soon a row had been formed up there on the platform, with tables and inkstands and tumblers of water; while we, many hundreds of us, scraped and shuffled and filled the entire body of some vast municipal building beneath. The proceedings somehow opened.

Perhaps an organ played. Perhaps songs were sung. Then the talking and the laughing suddenly subsided. A bell struck; a figure rose; a woman took her way from among us; she mounted a platform; she spoke for precisely five minutes; she descended. Directly she sat down another woman rose; mounted the platform; spoke for precisely five minutes and descended; then a third rose, then a fourth – and so it went on, speaker following speaker, one from the right, one from the left, one from the middle, one from the background – each took her way to the stand, said what she had to say, and gave place to her successor. There was something military in the regularity of the proceeding. They were like marksmen, I thought, standing up in turn with rifle raised to aim at a target. Sometimes they missed, and there was a roar of laughter; sometimes they hit, and there was a roar of applause. But whether the particular shot hit or missed there was no doubt about the carefulness of the aim. There was no beating the bush; there were no phrases of easy eloquence. The speaker made her way to the stand primed with her subject. Determination and resolution were stamped on her face. There was so much to be said between the strokes of the bell that she could not waste one second. The moment had come for which she had been waiting, perhaps for many months. The moment had come for which she had stored hat, shoes and dress – there was an air of discreet novelty about her clothing. But above all the moment had come when she was going to speak her mind, the mind of her constituency, the mind of the women who had sent her from Devonshire, perhaps, or Sussex, or some black mining village in Yorkshire to speak their mind for them in Newcastle.

It soon became obvious that the mind which lay spread over so wide a stretch of England was a vigorous mind working with great activity. It was thinking in June 1913 of the reform of the Divorce Laws; of the taxation of land values; of the Minimum

Wage. It was concerned with the Care of maternity; with the Trades Board Act; with the education of children over fourteen; it was unanimously of opinion that Adult Suffrage should become a Government measure – it was thinking in short about every sort of public question, and it was thinking constructively and pugnaciously. Accrington did not see eye to eye with Halifax, nor Middlesbrough with Plymouth. There was argument and opposition; resolutions were lost and amendments won. Hands shot up stiff as swords, or were pressed as stiffly to the side. Speaker followed speaker; the morning was cut up into precise lengths of five minutes by the bell.

Meanwhile – let me try after seventeen years to sum up the thoughts that passed through the minds of your guests, who had come from London and elsewhere, not to take part, but to listen – meanwhile what was it all about? What was the meaning of it? These women were demanding divorce, education, the vote – all good things. They were demanding higher wages and shorter hours – what could be more reasonable? And yet, though it was all so reasonable, much of it so forcible, some of it so humorous, a weight of discomfort was settling and shifting itself uneasily from side to side in your visitors' minds. All these questions – perhaps this was at the bottom of it – which matter so intensely to the people here, questions of sanitation and education and wages, this demand for an extra shilling, for another year at school, for eight hours instead of nine behind a counter or in a mill, leave me, in my own blood and bones, untouched. If every reform they demand was granted this very instant it would not touch one hair of my comfortable capitalistic head. Hence my interest is merely altruistic. It is thin spread and moon coloured. There is no life blood or urgency about it. However hard I clap my hands or stamp my feet there is a hollowness in the sound which betrays me. I am a benevolent spectator. I am irretrievably cut off from the actors. I sit here hypocritically clapping and stamping, an outcast from the flock. On top of this too, my reason (it was in 1913, remember) could not help assuring me that even if the resolution, whatever it was, were carried unanimously the stamping and the clapping was an empty noise. It would pass out of the open window and become part of the clamour of the lorries and the striving of the hooves on the cobbles of Newcastle beneath – an inarticulate uproar. The mind might be active; the mind might be aggressive; but the mind was without a body; it had no legs or arms with which to enforce its will. In all that audience, among all those women who worked, who bore children, who scrubbed and cooked and bargained, there was not a single woman with a vote. Let them fire off their rifles if they liked, but they would hit no target; there were only blank cartridges inside. The thought was irritating and depressing in the extreme.

The clock had now struck half-past eleven. Thus there were still then many hours to come. And if one had reached this stage of irritation and depression by half-past eleven in the morning, into what depths of boredom and despair would one not be plunged by half-past five in the evening? How could one sit out another day of speechifying? How could one, above all, face you, our hostess, with the information that your Congress had proved so insupportably exacerbating that one was going back to London by the very first train? The only chance lay in some happy conjuring trick, some change of attitude by which the mist and blankness of the speeches could be turned to blood and bone. Otherwise they remained intolerable. But suppose one played a childish game; suppose one said, as a child says, 'Let's pretend.' 'Let's pretend,' one said to oneself, looking at the speaker, 'that I am Mrs. Giles of Durham City.' A woman of that name had just turned to address us. 'I am the wife of a miner. He comes back thick with grime. First he must have his bath. Then he must have his supper. But there is only a copper.

My range is crowded with saucepans. There is no getting on with the work. All my crocks are covered with dust again. Why in the Lord's name have I not hot water and electric light laid on when middle-class women...' So up I jump and demand passionately 'labour saving appliances and housing reform.' Up I jump in the person of Mrs. Giles of Durham; in the person of Mrs. Phillips of Bacup; in the person of Mrs. Edwards of Wolverton. But after all the imagination is largely the child of the flesh. One could not be Mrs. Giles of Durham because one's body had never stood at the wash-tub; one's hands had never wrung and scrubbed and chopped up whatever the meat may be that makes a miner's supper. The picture therefore was always letting in irrelevancies. One sat in an armchair or read a book. One saw landscapes and seascapes, perhaps Greece or Italy, where Mrs. Giles or Mrs. Edwards must have seen slag heaps and rows upon rows of slate-roofed houses. Something was always creeping in from a world that was not their world and making the picture false and the game too much of a game to be worth playing.

It was true that one could always correct these fancy portraits by taking a look at the actual person – at Mrs. Thomas, or Mrs. Langrish, or Miss Bolt of Hebden Bridge. They were worth looking at. Certainly, there were no armchairs, or electric light, or hot water laid on in their lives; no Greek hills or Mediterranean bays in their dreams. Bakers and butchers did not call for orders. They did not sign a cheque to pay the weekly bills, or order, over the telephone, a cheap but quite adequate seat at the Opera. If they travelled it was on excursion day, with food in string bags and babies in their arms. They did not stroll through the house and say, that cover must go to the wash, or those sheets need changing. They plunged their arms in hot water and scrubbed the clothes themselves. In consequence their bodies were thick-set and muscular, their hands were large, and they had the slow emphatic gestures of people who are often stiff and fall tired in a heap on hard-backed chairs. They touched nothing lightly. They gripped papers and pencils as if they were brooms. Their faces were firm and heavily folded and lined with deep lines. It seemed as if their muscles were always taut and on the stretch. Their eyes looked as if they were always set on something actual – on saucepans that were boiling over, on children who were getting into mischief. Their lips never expressed the lighter and more detached emotions that come into play when the mind is perfectly at ease about the present. No, they were not in the least detached and easy and cosmopolitan. They were indigenous and rooted to one spot. Their very names were like the stones of the fields – common, grey, worn, obscure, docked of all splendours of association and romance. Of course they wanted baths and ovens and education and seventeen shillings instead of sixteen, and freedom and air and... 'And,' said Mrs. Winthrop of Spennymoor, breaking into these thoughts with words that sounded like a refrain, 'we can wait.' ... 'Yes,' she repeated, as if she had waited so long that the last lap of that immense vigil meant nothing for the end was in sight, 'we can wait.' And she got down rather stiffly from her perch and made her way back to her seat, an elderly woman dressed in her best clothes.

Then Mrs. Potter spoke. Then Mrs. Elphick. Then Mrs. Holmes of Edgbaston. So it went on, and at last after innumerable speeches, after many communal meals at long tables and many arguments – the world was to be reformed, from top to bottom, in a variety of ways – after seeing Co-operative jams bottled and Co-operative biscuits made, after some song singing and ceremonies with banners, the new President received the chain of office with a kiss from the old President; the Congress dispersed; and the separate members who had stood up so valiantly and spoken out so boldly while the clock ticked its five minutes went back to Yorkshire and Wales and Sussex and Devonshire, and hung their clothes in the wardrobe and plunged their hands in the wash-tub again.

Later that summer the thoughts here so inadequately described, were again discussed, but not in a public hall hung with banners and loud with voices. The head office of the Guild, the centre from which speakers, papers, inkstands and tumblers, as I suppose, issued, was then in Hampstead. There, if I may remind you again of what you may well have forgotten, you invited us to come; you asked us to tell you how the Congress had impressed us. But I must pause on the threshold of that very dignified old house, with its eighteenth-century carvings and panelling, as we paused then in truth, for one could not enter and go upstairs without encountering Miss Kidd. Miss Kidd sat at her typewriter in the outer office. Miss Kidd, one felt, had set herself as a kind of watch-dog to ward off the meddle-some middle-class wasters of time who come prying into other people's business. Whether it was for this reason that she was dressed in a peculiar shade of deep purple I do not know. The colour seemed somehow symbolical. She was very short, but, owing to the weight which sat on her brow and the gloom which seemed to issue from her dress, she was also very heavy. An extra share of the world's grievances seemed to press upon her shoulders. When she clicked her typewriter one felt that she was making that instrument transmit messages of foreboding and ill-omen to an unheeding universe. But she relented, and like all relentings after gloom hers came with a sudden charm. Then we went upstairs, and upstairs we came upon a very different figure – upon Miss Lilian Harris, indeed, who, whether it was due to her dress which was coffee coloured, or to her smile which was serene, or to the ash-tray in which many cigarettes had come amiably to an end, seemed the image of detachment and equanimity. Had one not known that Miss Harris was to the

Congress what the heart is to the remoter veins – that the great engine at Newcastle would not have thumped and throbbed without her – that she had collected and sorted and summoned and arranged that very intricate but orderly assembly of women – she would never have enlightened one. She had nothing whatever to do; she licked a few stamps and addressed a few envelopes – it was a fad of hers – that was what her manner conveyed. It was Miss Harris who moved the papers off the chairs and got the tea-cups out of the cupboard. It was she who answered questions about figures and put her hand on the right file of letters infallibly and sat listening, without saying very much, but with calm comprehension, to whatever was said.

Again let me telescope into a few sentences, and into one scene many random discussions on various occasions at various places. We said then – for you now emerged from an inner room, and if Miss Kidd was purple and Miss Harris was coffee coloured, you, speaking pictorially (and I dare not speak more explicitly) were kingfisher blue and as arrowy and decisive as that quick bird – we said then that the Congress had roused thoughts and ideas of the most diverse nature. It had been a revelation and a disillusionment. We had been humiliated and enraged. To begin with, all their talk, we said, or the greater part of it, was of matters of fact. They want baths and money. To expect us, whose minds, such as they are, fly free at the end of a short length of capital to tie ourselves down again to that narrow plot of acquisitiveness and desire is impossible. We have baths and we have money. Therefore, however much we had sympathised our sympathy was largely fictitious. It was aesthetic sympathy, the sympathy of the eye and of the imagination, not of the heart and of the nerves; and such sympathy is always physically uncomfortable. Let us explain what we mean, we said. The Guild's women are magnificent to look at. Ladies in evening dress are lovelier far, but they lack the sculpturesque quality that these working women have. And though the range of expression is narrower in working women, their few expressions have a force and an emphasis, of tragedy or humour, which the faces of ladies lack. But, at the same time, it is much better to be a lady; ladies desire Mozart and Einstein – that is, they desire things that are ends, not things that are means. Therefore to deride ladies and to imitate, as some of the speakers did, their mincing speech and little knowledge of what it pleases them to call 'reality' is, so it seems to us, not merely foolish but gives away the whole purpose of the Congress, for if it is better to be working women by all means let them remain so and not undergo the contamination which wealth and comfort bring. In spite of this, we went on, apart from prejudice and bandying compliments, undoubtedly the women at the Congress possess something which ladies lack, and something which is desirable, which is stimulating, and yet very difficult to define. One does not want to slip easily into fine phrases about 'contact with life,' about 'facing facts' and 'the teaching of experience,' for they invariably alienate the hearer, and moreover no working man or woman works harder or is in closer touch with reality than a painter with his brush or a writer with his pen. But the quality that they have, judging from a phrase caught here and there, from a laugh, or a gesture seen in passing, is precisely the quality that Shakespeare would have enjoyed. One can fancy him slipping away from the brilliant salons of educated people to crack a joke in Mrs. Robson's back kitchen. Indeed, we said, one of our most curious impressions at your Congress was that the 'poor,' 'the working classes,' or by whatever name you choose to call them, are not downtrodden, envious and exhausted; they are humorous and vigorous and thoroughly independent. Thus if it were possible to meet them not as masters or mistresses or customers with a counter between us, but over the wash-tub or in the parlour casually and congenially as fellow-beings with the same wishes and ends in view, a great liberation would follow, and perhaps friendship and sympathy would supervene. How many words must lurk in those women's vocabularies that have faded from ours! How many scenes must lie dormant in their eye which are unseen by ours! What images and saws and proverbial sayings must still be current with them that have never reached the surface of print, and very likely they still keep the power which we have lost of making new ones. There were many shrewd sayings in the speeches at Congress which even the weight of a public meeting could not flatten out entirely. But, we said, and here perhaps fiddled with a paper knife, or poked the fire impatiently by way of expressing our discontent, what is the use of it all? Our sympathy is fictitious, not real. Because the baker calls and we pay our bills with cheques, and our clothes are washed for us and we do not know the liver from the lights we are condemned to remain forever shut up in the confines of the middle classes, wearing tail coats and silk stockings, and called Sir or Madam as the case may be, when we are all, in truth, simply Johns and Susans. And they remain equally deprived. For we have as much to give them as they to give us – wit and detachment, learning and poetry, and all those good gifts which those who have never answered bells or minded machines enjoy by right. But the barrier is impassable. And nothing perhaps exacerbated us more at the Congress (you must have noticed at times a certain irritability) than the thought that this force of theirs, this smouldering heat which broke the crust now and then and licked the surface with a hot and fearless flame, is about to break through and melt us together so that life will be richer and books more complex and society will pool its possessions instead of segregating them – all this is going to happen inevitably, thanks to you, very largely, and to Miss Harris and to Miss Kidd – but only when we are dead.

It was thus that we tried in the Guild Office that afternoon to explain the nature of fictitious sympathy and how it differs from real sympathy and how defective it is because it is not based upon sharing the same important emotions unconsciously. It was thus that we tried to describe the contradictory and complex feelings which beset the middle-class visitor when forced to sit out a Congress of working women in silence.

Perhaps it was at this point that you unlocked a drawer and took out a packet of papers. You did not at once untie the string that fastened them. Sometimes, you said, you got a letter which you could not bring yourself to burn; once or twice a Guildswoman had at your suggestion written a few pages about her life. It might be that we should find these papers interesting; that if we read them the women would cease to be symbols and would become instead individuals. But they were very fragmentary and ungrammatical; they had been jotted down in the intervals of housework. Indeed you could not at once bring yourself to give them up, as if to expose them to other eyes were a breach of confidence. It might be that their crudity would only perplex, that the writing of people who do not know how to write – but at this point we burst in. In the first place, every Englishwoman knows how to write; in the second, even if she does not she has only to take her own life for subject and write the truth about that and not fiction or poetry for our interest to be so keenly roused that – that in short we cannot wait but must read the packet at once.

Thus pressed you did by degrees and with many delays – there was the war for example, and Miss Kidd died, and you and Lilian Harris retired from the Guild, and a testimonial was given you in a casket, and many thousands of working women tried to say how you had changed their lives – tried to say what they will feel for you to their dying day – after all these interruptions you did at last gather the papers together and finally put them in my hands early this May. There they were, typed and docketed with a few snapshots and rather faded photographs stuck between the pages. And when at last I began to read, there started up in my mind's eye the figures that I had seen all those years ago at Newcastle with such bewilderment and curiosity. But they were no longer addressing a large meeting in Newcastle from a platform, dressed in their best clothes. The hot June day with its banners and its ceremonies had vanished, and instead one looked back into the past of the women who had stood there; into the four-roomed houses of miners, into the homes of small shopkeepers and agricultural labourers, into the fields and factories of fifty or sixty years ago. Mrs. Burrows, for example, had worked in the Lincolnshire fens when she was eight with forty or fifty other children, and an old man had followed the gang with a long whip in his hand 'which he did not forget to use.' That was a strange reflection. Most of the women had started work at seven or eight, earning a penny on Saturday for washing a doorstep, or twopence a week for carrying suppers to the men at the iron foundry. They had gone into factories when they were fourteen. They had worked from seven in the morning till eight or nine at night and had made thirteen or fifteen shillings a week. Out of this money they had saved some pence with which to buy their mother gin – she was often very tired in the evening and had borne perhaps thirteen children in as many years; or they fetched opium to assuage some miserable old woman's ague in the fens. Old Betty Rollett killed herself when she could get no more. They had seen half-starved women standing in rows to be paid for their matchboxes while they snuffed the roast meat of their employer's dinner cooking within. The smallpox had raged in Bethnal Green and they had known that the boxes went on being made in the sick-room and were sold to the public with the infection still thick on them. They had been so cold working in the wintry fields that they could not run when the ganger gave them leave. They had waded through floods when the Wash overflowed its banks. Kind old ladies had given them parcels of food which had turned out to contain only crusts of bread and rancid bacon rind. All this they had done and seen and known when other children were still dabbling in seaside pools and spelling out fairy tales by the nursery fire. Naturally their faces had a different look on them. But they were, one remembered, firm faces, faces with something indomitable in their expression. Astonishing though it seems, human nature is so tough that it will take such wounds, even at the tenderest age, and survive them. Keep a child mewed in Bethnal Green and she will somehow snuff the country air from seeing the yellow dust on her brother's boots, and nothing will serve her but she must go there and see the 'clean ground,' as she calls it, for herself. It was true that at first the 'bees were very frightening,' but all the same she got to the country and the blue smoke and the cows came up to her expectation. Put girls, after a childhood of minding smaller brothers and washing doorsteps, into a factory when they are fourteen and their eyes will turn to the window and they will be happy because, as the workroom is six storeys high, the sun can be seen breaking over the hills, 'and that was always such a comfort and help.' Still stranger, if one needs additional proof of the strength of the human instinct to escape from bondage and attach itself whether to a country road or to a sunrise over the hills, is the fact that the highest ideals of duty flourish, in an obscure hat factory as surely as on a battlefield. There were women in Christies' felt hat factory, for example, who worked for 'honour.' They gave their lives to the cause of putting straight stitches into the bindings of men's hat brims. Felt is hard and thick; it is difficult to push the needle through; there are no rewards or glory to be won; but such is the incorrigible idealism of the human mind that there were 'trimmers' in those obscure places who would never put a crooked stitch in their work and ruthlessly tore out the crooked stitches of others. And as they drove in their straight stitches they reverenced Queen Victoria and thanked God, drawing up to the fire, that they were all married to good Conservative working men.

Certainly that story explained something of the force, of the obstinacy, which one had seen in the faces of the speakers at Newcastle. And then, if one went on reading these papers, one came upon other signs of the extraordinary vitality of the human spirit. That inborn energy which no amount of child-birth and washing up can quench had reached out, it seemed, and seized upon old copies of magazines; had attached itself to Dickens; had propped the poems of Burns against a dish cover to read while cooking. They read at meals; they read before going to the mill. They read Dickens and Scott and Henry George and Bulwer Lytton and Ella Wheeler Wilcox and Alice Meynell and would like 'to get hold of any good history of the French Revolution, not Carlyle's, please,' and B. Russell on China, and William Morris and Shelley and Florence Barclay and Samuel Butler's Note Books – they read with the indiscriminate greed of a hungry appetite, that crams itself with toffee and beef and tarts and vinegar and champagne all in one gulp. Naturally such reading led to argument. The younger generation had the audacity to say that Queen Victoria was no better than an honest charwoman who had brought up her children respectably. They had the temerity to doubt whether to sew straight stitches into men's hat brims should be the sole aim and end of a woman's life. They started arguments and even held rudimentary debating societies on the floor of the factory. In time the old trimmers even were shaken in their beliefs and came to think that there might be other ideals in the world besides straight stitches and Queen Victoria. Strange ideas indeed were seething in their brain. A girl, for instance, would reason, as she walked along the streets of a factory town, that she had no right to bring a child into the world if that child must earn its living in a mill. A chance saying in a book would fire her imagination to dream of future cities where there were to be baths and kitchens and washhouses and art galleries and museums and parks. The minds of working women were humming and their imaginations were awake. But how were they to realise their ideals? How were they to express their needs? It was hard enough for middle class women with some amount of money and some degree of education behind them. But how could women whose hands were full of work, whose kitchens were thick with steam, who had neither education nor encouragement nor leisure remodel the world according to the ideas of working women? It was then, I suppose, sometime in the eighties, that the Women's Guild crept modestly and tentatively into existence. For a time it occupied an inch or two of space in the *Co-operative News* which called itself The Women's Corner. It was there that Mrs. Acland asked, 'Why should we not hold our Co-operative mothers' meetings, when we may bring our work and sit together, one of us reading some Co-operative work aloud, which may afterwards be discussed?' And on April 18th, 1883, she announced that the Women's Guild now numbered seven members. It was the Guild then that drew to itself all that restless wishing and dreaming. It was the Guild that made a central meeting place where formed and solidified all that was else so scattered and incoherent. The Guild must have given the older women, with their husbands and children, what 'clean ground' had given to the little girl in Bethnal Green, or the view of day breaking over the hills had given the girls in the hat factory. It gave them in the first place the rarest of all possessions – a room where they could sit down and think remote from boiling saucepans and crying children; and then that room became not merely a sitting-room and a meeting place, but a workshop where, laying their heads together, they could remodel their houses, could remodel their lives, could beat out this reform and that. And, as the membership grew, and twenty or thirty women made a practice of meeting weekly, so their ideas increased, and their interests widened. Instead of discussing merely their own taps and their own sinks and their own long hours and little pay, they began to discuss education and taxation and the conditions of work in the country at large. The women who had crept modestly in 1883 into Mrs. Acland's sitting-room to sew and 'read some Co-operative work aloud,' learnt to speak out, boldly and authoritatively, about every question of civic life. Thus it came about that Mrs. Robson and Mrs. Potter and Mrs. Wright at Newcastle in 1913 were asking not only for baths and wages and electric light, but also for adult suffrage and the taxation of land values and divorce law reform. Thus in a year or two they were to demand peace and disarmament and the spread of Co-operative principles, not only among the working people of Great Britain, but among the nations of the world. And the force that lay behind their speeches and drove them home beyond the reach of eloquence was compact of many things – of men with whips, of sick rooms where match-boxes were made, of hunger and cold, of many and difficult child-births, of much scrubbing and washing up, of reading Shelley and William Morris and Samuel Butler over the kitchen table, of weekly meetings of the Women's Guild, of Committees and Congresses at Manchester and elsewhere. All this lay behind the speeches of Mrs. Robson and Mrs. Potter and Mrs. Wright. The papers which you sent me certainly threw some light upon the old curiosities and bewilderments which had made that Congress so memorable, and so thick with un-answered questions.

But that the pages here printed should mean all this to those who cannot supplement the written word with the memory of faces and the sound of voices is perhaps unlikely. It cannot be denied that the chapters here put together do not make a book – that as literature they have many limitations. The writing, a literary critic might say, lacks detachment and imaginative breadth, even as the women themselves lacked variety and play of feature. Here are no reflections, he might object, no view of life as a whole, and no attempt to enter into the lives of other people. Poetry and fiction seem far beyond their horizon. Indeed, we are reminded of those obscure writers before the birth of Shakespeare who never travelled beyond the borders of their own parishes, who read no language but their own, and wrote with difficulty, finding few words and those awkwardly. And yet since writing is a complex art, much infected by life, these pages have some qualities even as literature that the literate and instructed might envy. Listen, for instance, to Mrs. Scott, the felt hat worker:

> I have been over the hilltops when the snow drifts were over three feet high, and six feet in some places. I was in a blizzard in Hayfield and thought I should never get round the corners. But it was life on the moors; I seemed to know every blade of grass and where the flowers grew and all the little streams were my companions.

Could she have said that better if Oxford had made her a Doctor of Letters? Or take Mrs. Layton's description of a matchbox factory in Bethnal Green and how she looked through the fence and saw three ladies 'sitting in the shade doing some kind of fancy work.' It has something of the accuracy and clarity of a description by Defoe. And when Mrs. Burrows brings to mind that bitter day when the children were about to eat their cold dinner and drink their cold tea under the hedge and the ugly woman asked them into her parlour saying, 'Bring these children into my house and let them eat their dinner there,' the words are simple, but it is difficult to see how they could say more. And then there is a fragment of a letter from Miss Kidd – the sombre purple figure who typed as if the weight of the world were on her shoulders. 'When I was a girl of seventeen,' she writes,

> my then employer, a gentleman of good position and high standing in the town, sent me to his home one night, ostensibly to take a parcel of books, but really with a very different object. When I arrived at the house all the family were away, and before he would allow me to leave he forced me to yield to him. At eighteen I was a mother.

Whether that is literature or not literature I do not presume to say, but that it explains much and reveals much is certain. Such then was the burden that rested on that sombre figure as she sat typing your letters, such were the memories she brooded as she guarded your door with her grim and indomitable fidelity.

But I will quote no more. These pages are only fragments. These voices are beginning only now to emerge from silence into half articulate speech. These lives are still half hidden in profound obscurity. To express even what is expressed here has been a work of labour and difficulty. The writing has been done in kitchens, at odds and ends of leisure, in the midst of distractions and obstacles – but really there is no need for me, in a letter addressed to you, to lay stress upon the hardship of working women's lives. Have not you and Lilian Harris given your best years – but hush! you will not let me finish that sentence and therefore, with the old messages of friendship and admiration, I will make an end.

May 1930.

Dreadnought Notes (1940)

… We were told that the best thing we could do was to go to Mr McKenna who was then First Lord of the Admiralty and make a clean breast of it. We were told by a friend of Mr McKenna's that if we took all the blame on ourselves they would not take any steps against the admiral or the other officers. The House of Commons would be told that we had apologised and there would be an end of it. So my brother and Duncan Grant went to the Admiralty and were shown in to Mr McKenna. And there they had a very queer interview. They tried to explain that they didn't want to get the admiral into trouble; and Mr McKenna dismissed the idea that such foolish people could get so great a man into a scrape, and pointed out that one of them had committed a forgery and was liable to go to gaol. So they argued at loggerheads. The truth was I think that Mr McKenna was secretly a good deal amused, and liked the hoax, but didn't want it repeated. At any rate he treated them as if they were school boys, and told them not to do it again. But we heard afterwards that one result of our visit had been that the regulations were tightened up; and that rules were made about telegrams that make it almost impossible now to repeat the joke. I am glad to think that I too have been of help to my country.

With that interview with the First Lord of the Admiralty we hoped that the affair was over. But no – there was still the navy to reckon with. I was just getting out of bed one Sunday morning soon afterwards when there was a ring at the bell; and then I heard a man's voice downstairs. I seemed to recognise the voice. It was my cousin's. It was Willy Fisher. And though I could not hear what he said I could tell that he was saying something very forcible. At last the voices ceased and my brother appeared. He was in his dressing gown. He looked very upset. And he told me that Willy Fisher had been in a towering rage; had said he had found out who we were. And he was horrified. Did we realise that all the little boys ran after Admiral May in the street calling out Bunga Bunga? Did we realise that we owed our lives to the British Navy? Did we realise that we were impertinent, idiotic? Did we realise that we ought to be whipped through the streets, did we realise that if we had been discovered we should have been stripped naked and thrown into the sea? And so on and so on. My brother thought he was going to whip a knife out of his sleeve and proceed to blows. But no, Willy Fisher explained that since my brother's mother was his own Aunt, the rules of the Navy forbade any actual physical punishment. Then he asked: 'I know who the others were; and now you've got to tell me their addresses.' This my brother did. The next moment he realised his mistake. But it was too late. And Willy Fisher dashed out of the house brushing aside the hand which my brother – who was after all his first cousin – held out to him.

We hadn't long to wait before we heard what happened next. Three naval officers were waiting outside in a taxi. They drove off to the address in Hampstead where Duncan Grant lived. Duncan Grant was just sitting down to breakfast with his father and mother. They sent word that a friend was outside and wished to speak to him. Duncan Grant got up and went down into the street. One of the young men tipped him up and flung him head foremost into the taxi. Mrs Grant who was looking out of the window saw her son disappear head foremost and turned back in alarm. 'What on earth are we to do' she asked her husband. 'Someone's kidnapping Duncan.' Major Grant who had been in the army himself merely smiled and said 'I expect it's his friends from the Dreadnought.'

Duncan Grant found that he was sitting on the floor at the feet of three large men who carried a bundle of canes. Duncan asked where they were taking him? 'You'll see plenty of Dreadnoughts where you're going' said Willy Fisher. At last they stopped somewhere in a lonely part of Hampstead Heath. They all got out. Duncan Grant stood there like a lamb. It was useless to fight. They were three against one. And this rather upset them. 'I can't make this chap out' said one of the officers. He doesn't put up any fight. You cant cane a chap like that.' My cousin however ordered them to proceed. He was too high in the service to lend a hand himself. And so, very reluctantly, one of the junior officers took a cane and gave Duncan Grant two ceremonial taps. Then they said the honour of the navy was avenged. There was Duncan Grant standing without a hat in his bedroom slippers. They at once conceived an affection for him and I am not surprised. They were really sorry for him. 'You can't go home like that' they said. But Duncan Grant felt that he would much rather go home in the tube in his slippers than be driven back by the officers. And so he shuffled off; and the officers disappeared in their car...

There is only one thing to add. About a week or two later the real Emperor of Abyssinia arrived in London. He complained that wherever he went in the street boys ran after him calling out Bunga Bunga. And when he asked the first Lord of the Admiralty whether he might visit the Channel Fleet, Mr McKenna replied that he regretted to inform his Majesty that it was quite impossible.

Interview (1910)

'I had only two days' notice of the adventure,' she said, 'and I entered into it because I thought I would like the fun.

'I felt rather nervous until I got in the train at Paddington. Although I wore a false beard and moustache and a wig and a turban and flowing robes, I could not realise that no one would recognise me. When we got into the special saloon of the train my nervousness disappeared, and I felt that it did not matter what happened.

'We were received at Weymouth by the flag lieutenant, who gravely saluted us, and then we were taken to the Dreadnought in the admiral's pinnace.

'So far everything had worked perfectly. I spoke as little as possible in case my voice, which I made as gruff as I could, should fail me. I found I could easily laugh like a man, but it was difficult to disguise the speaking voice.

'As a matter of fact, the really only trying time I had was when I had to shake hands with my first cousin, who is an officer on the Dreadnought, and who saluted me as I went on deck. I thought I should burst out laughing, but, happily, I managed to preserve my Oriental stolidity of countenance.

'There were some amusing incidents on the return journey. Mr. Cholmondely [Cole] gravely told the railway officials that the princes could not have any meals served with the naked hand. There were no spare gloves on the train, and the officials consequently had to buy a few pairs, and the attendants who waited on us at dinner appeared wearing grey kid gloves. We gave them princely tips.

'Prince Maketen [sic], the chief, had a very bad cold. He had trouble with his nose and face all day, and the twitching of his face had been so constant that during dinner half his moustache fell off. Fortunately none of the state servants saw the accident, or the game would have been up.

'Taking off my beard and moustache after I reached home was a long operation. They were gummed on, and I thought my face would never feel clean again. The powder soon came off, and so did the wig.'

[From a photograph by Sinnett (Burton-on-Trent)

A CONGRESS OF THE WOMEN'S CO-OPERATIVE GUILD

9. A congress of the Women's Co-operative Guild.

"THE EMPEROR OF ABYSSINIA" AND HIS SUITE.

Names from left to right:

Virginia Stephen, Duncan Grant, Adrian Stephen, Anthony Buxton,
Guy Ridley, Horace Cole.

10. The *Dreadnought* Hoax.

V
Memoir Fantasies

'Oh Miss Genia, Miss Genia!' exclaimed the Stephen family cook (Quentin Bell remembered Virginia Woolf's telling) as Virginia Stephen returned in blackface and beard from the *Dreadnought* Hoax. That cook – Sophia Farrell – was the subject of one of three pieces Woolf wrote after the biographical fantasy *Orlando* and then left unpublished in various states of revision. The sketches of Sophie (or Sophy) Farrell, Saxon Sydney-Turner and John Maynard Keynes could all be called fantasy memoirs. They are recollections of living people Woolf knew well, and whose lives she briefly recounted and fictionalised with disguised names or initials. The memoir forms of the sketches vary considerably. That of the cook is a realistic narrative, 'One of Our Great Men' is ironic, and the life of Keynes is elliptical and comic. Throughout her career in both her essays and her novels, Virginia Woolf speculated on what, in an early letter, she called 'the proper writing of lives' (15th April 1908). It was indeed a Bloomsbury theme, most famously shown in the ironic lives of Lytton Strachey's *Eminent Victorians*. Woolf was intrigued by the boundaries of biography and autobiography, beginning with comic lives of friends and relatives that mixed fiction in with fact. (The one of Caroline Emelia Stephen has not, alas, survived.)

The sketch titled 'The Cook' is a reminiscence of the Stephen family cook of more than fifty years. The form of the reminiscence is fiction, but the content is factual apart from the made-up names. Sophie became the Stephen cook in 1886, when she was twenty-five. She remained after Julia Stephen's death (a draft of the cook has 'the Master' asking her to promise never to leave) and moved to Bloomsbury with the family after Leslie Stephen's death. When Vanessa married Clive Bell Sophie went with Virginia and Adrian Stephen to be their cook, and there she was when Virginia returned from the *Dreadnought* Hoax. 'The Cook' is the only one of the three fantasy memoirs in which Virginia represents herself: she is Ursula (an allusion perhaps to the British saint of the 11,000 virgins?) who is 'such a harum scarum thing – she wouldn't know if they sold her'. After Virginia's marriage Sophie cooked for various other members of the family, refusing later to join the Woolfs' household. When she eventually retired she was partly pensioned by Virginia.

Around the time she sketched Sophie, Virginia was writing about her Co-operative working women. Several years later after a Co-operative conference she described the women in her diary as 'fine old housekeepers; of the Sophie type; massive, determined' (20th June 1933). Sophie's career is also reflected to some extent in the servant Crosby of Woolf's novel *The Years* (1937). Memories of Sophie reappear later in 'Sketch of the Past', where she is portrayed again as a dominant kitchen force on whose moods food baskets let down outside from the children's bedrooms depended. Sophie's determination is most sadly shown in her refusal to marry because she considered herself illegitimate. The marriage of her parents in France was not recognised in Britain, because her mother was the sister of her father's late wife.

'The Cook' is the most straightforwardly presented of Woolf's three fantasy memoirs, the one in which the subject is most clearly dramatised and of a quite different class, of course, than the other two. It also has the longest vistas from the platform of the present on which the memoir ends. For the reader the vista can extend into the future with the words Sophie Farrell sent to Leonard Woolf after Virginia's suicide:

I have known and loved her Very Much, Eversince she was 4 years old. I can't bear to feel She has Strayed away from you all.

In *Orlando* Virginia Woolf had thanked Saxon Sydney-Turner for his 'wide and peculiar erudition [which] has saved me, I hope, some lamentable blunders'. No one who knew Saxon doubted the depth or the peculiarity of his knowledge, which in 'One of Our Great Men' extends from Greek to puzzles, horses and rabbits. That Virginia based F.A.R. Rankin on Saxon is not in doubt. (Quentin Bell in his biography of Woolf describes him with a quotation from the sketch.) Yet the memoir is also a fantasy. When she wrote it sometime in the 1930s, Sydney-Turner was still working in the Treasury and did not retire until well after her death. Still, there are numerous connections between Rankin and Saxon, whose father, a doctor, ran a home for mental patients near Brighton, for instance. Sydney-Turner came into Bloomsbury and Virginia Stephen's life through his close friendship at Cambridge with her brother Thoby Stephen, with Lytton Strachey and with Leonard Woolf, all of whom were less academically successful than the erudite Saxon. Thoby's early death strengthened Saxon's friendship with Virginia – he was even rather incredibly thought of as a suitor for her by some friends.

Virginia Woolf's memoir fantasy of Saxon Sydney-Turner may be partly based on quite a different kind of sketch, one in a series that Leonard Woolf wrote around the time he married Virginia (one of them was of herself). Much later Leonard reprinted the sketch in his autobiography. There he describes Saxon as a cocooned Aristotle endlessly spinning webs of the past over the present that desecrate even literature. In his less imaginative autobiographical recollections of Saxon, Leonard described his odd gliding walk (he flits in Virginia's sketch), and his uncreative brilliance. He put Saxon into his novel *The Wise Virgins* (1913), and when he wrote an obituary letter to *The Times* after Saxon's death in 1962, Leonard described him as 'an eccentric in the best English tradition' who wrote elegant verse and music and possessed 'an extraordinarily supple, and enigmatic mind'. There is nothing in Virginia's sketch about

Saxon's musical obsessions (especially Wagner) but the enigma of his mind is apparent. 'One of Our Great Men' is a distancing, ironic memoir, largely reflecting the views of his friends. The amusing incongruity of their expectations and Rankin's achievements is left unresolved by the non-committal narrator.

It is difficult to find a greater contrast in the subjects of Virginia Woolf's brief memoirs than the obscure Saxon Sydney-Turner and the world-famous John Maynard Keynes, both of whom worked in the Treasury. (Keynes described Saxon with admirable understatement as a 'quietist'.) In the spring of 1934 Virginia Woolf jotted down the initials JMK at the top of a page in one of her writing notebooks. Under them she rapidly wrote a three-page biographical sketch on themes in the current life of John Maynard Keynes. The sketch connects two of the most remarkable members of Bloomsbury as well as illustrating in miniature Woolf's interest in 'the proper writing of lives'.

Admiration and affection mingle with irony in Virginia Woolf's sketch. She begins with a list of topics in the life of JMK, but develops only half a dozen or so of them. From a pig and a college, the memoir fantasy modulates to Covent Garden and Downing Street, mixes finance with book-collecting, and ends with the famous man in bed enquiring after a rare pamphlet and thinking of his engagements, of Atlantis and of the symbols that will eventually answer all problems. The transitions are rapid, sometimes abrupt or ironic, the shifting viewpoint both impersonal and internal. The absence of explanatory information combines with some very specific facts. Humour in the narrative ranges from understatement to hyperbole, and interconnections are suggested between the pig and the sausage being eaten, the mysterious criss-cross of the plan in the dust and the plan of the ballet as well as the frolicking xs and ys on the board.

The sudden dislocations of Woolf's short narrative are explained parenthetically and apologetically at the start by the 'infancy' of biographical art itself, which cannot proceed without the 'leading strings' that the narrator fails for the most part to provide here. Once again, Virginia Woolf reflects on the nature of memoir writing itself.

When Woolf's biographical fantasy of Keynes is examined closely, the factual basis of much of it emerges. Virginia sometimes thought of her novels in terms of fact and vision. 'JMK' is a work of Virginia Woolf's imagination, but the memoir of John Maynard Keynes in 1933 shows that much of what is visionary in it consists of the way the factual is treated. Keynes, for example, had become interested in pigs as Bursar at King's College and began breeding them at his country home near Charleston. A don but never a professor, he was even before his marriage an enthusiast of ballet and a financial advisor to the government. The very specific date of 15th June reflects events in Keynes's life during this month in 1933. The World Economic Conference was meeting in London that June; it included a gala performance by the Camargo Society organised by Keynes, in which his wife, the ballerina Lydia Lopokova, danced. The Queen attended the gala – and so did Virginia Woolf. The Conference was concerned with the stabilisation of currency exchanges, and Keynes was being consulted by Downing Street in the negotiations. Again in 1933, Keynes received from his brother a very rare abstract of the philosopher David Hume's *A Treatise on Human Nature* (but the two other known copies of the pamphlet were not in California and the Kremlin). There are further references in the sketch to Keynes's collection of works by British philosophers and economists, to his habit of working in bed in the mornings, to the centenary meetings of the Royal Statistical Society also in the summer of 1933, and to the Cézanne still life of seven (not five) apples that Keynes had bought in Paris during the war and hidden in the hedge at Charleston. Atlantis, it seems, was not one of Keynes's interests, though he made a hobby of studying the currencies of ancient civilisations. Finally, the juggle of cryptic symbols that will produce the one simple, sufficient and comprehensive word alludes fantastically to the great *General Theory of Employment, Interest and Money* that Keynes was writing in 1933 and would publish three years later, revolution-ising modern economics.

The memoir fantasy ends with a beginning and has a completeness that indicates 'JMK' is not a fragmentary com-position. The memoir stops again, like that of 'The Cook', on the platform of the present.

The Cook (1929?)

Her name was Biddy Brien. It had been O'Brien, but it lost the O when her father crossed the Channel in the early days of Queen Victoria. He was a farm labourer in Lincolnshire. Biddy was the eldest of a family of ten.

She had no schooling – it was before the days of compulsory education. She couldnt read and she couldnt write. Through her father she went back to the black days of famine. She remembered children whipped to work in the fields & remembered the rick burners – how she was called from her bed in the middle of the night, 'being no bigger than yourself' i.e. about the height of the kitchen table and set to hand buckets in a long chain of men women and children... (She could remember the light of the burning ricks flaring on their cottage...) Another anecdote was about a dry biscuit. They never actually 'went without' as she put it, still, they were hungry; and 'the old gentleman' – that is the rector, whose milk she brought daily, 'called me into his study and gave me' here she made a face 'a dry biscuit'. But her mother never let them go out with a hole in their stockings...

She went to service when she was a child. Her father promised her a silver watch if she kept the same place till she was eighteen. But she couldnt... 'The Mistress never gave us a kind word' she said.

She came to try her fortune in London. There she stood in answer to Mrs Savery's advertisement for a cook – a funny little squat girl, as neat as a new pin, with cheeks like red apples and a scar over one eye. She made up her mind on the instant – this was the place for her... 'There was your mother, and the six of you tumbling down the stairs after her...' She has often described the first sight of that family with whom she was to spend the whole of her working life... Instantly she conceived a passion for Mrs Savery.

But she was not an easy person to have in the kitchen. Her temper was violent. It was like a gale in the house – the doors slammed, the windows banged. On the other hand she could be as sunny as a summer morning... Mrs Savery had a temper too... But at a pinch, if there was illness, if twenty people sat down to dinner as they did sometimes, then she was as sunny as a summer morning. She sang like a bird among her pots and pans.

She had a passion for Mrs S & the children. But one summer something awful happened – even the children were aware of it. Biddy grew thin; she rocked over the fire as if she had the toothache. All the children knew was that 'they mustnt bother Biddy'... When they let down the basket over the Kitchen window, for scraps from the grown up dinner party, the string was cut short... It was only years later that they knew Biddy's secret, why she, with her passion for children, hadnt married. She almost broke her heart for the handsome postman. And he for her. Nothing would persuade her to marry an honest man. Why? Because she hadn't her marriage lines. 'What on earth d'you mean, Biddy?' her mistress asked. And so it came out – how her father had married his deceased wife's sister. Incredible though it seemed, he had crossed to France; he had married her there; but it was no use. The children were illegitimate. She hadnt her married lines. 'But he'll break his heart' Mrs Savery persisted. It was no good. There were things Biddy would not do.

Every year she had a fortnight's holiday in August when the family were away. One year she asked, might she take her holiday at Easter? 'But Biddy' said Mrs Savery, 'That'll be a little awkward...' Biddy stood her ground. It must be Easter this year. It was Holy Year. She was a Catholic. She was going to Rome to see the Pope.

'To Rome?' Mrs Savery was aghast. 'What about the fare?' Oh she'd saved up... out of wages that were £26 a year.

So she went to Rome. She saw the Pope. But Mrs Savery was dead before she came back. Biddy never forgave herself. 'Oh' she wailed, 'if I hadnt gone, it wouldnt have happened.' She would never never leave them again.

She ruled the kitchen... Other servants might complain. Somehow she taught herself to read. Her favourite book strangely enough was Rasselas. As for writing, she never mastered grammar; her spelling was done by ear. But all the same, her letters used to be read aloud in the family... Her standards were absolute. The ending was always the same; Your obedient and affectionate old servant... Her sayings used to be repeated. 'If you dont like it you must loomp it'... 'What you save on food you spend on doctors bills.' It almost broke her heart when she had to use cooking eggs during the war. She could 'go without'; but not the family. Her standards were very high for them. 'Oh Miss Ursula – it's not right for your mother's daughter to be seen,...' she would begin. She would leave the sentence unfinished. But it was enough... Miss Ursula and Miss Kate and Miss Ann, Master John and Master Richard, and Master Hugh didnt dare, so they always said, to face old Biddy. When they married, their first thought, so they said was, will Biddy like him or her? She had a way of summing you up, with her very blue eyes, and her silence... Nobody has ever been able to say so much by saying nothing. As she grew old, she grew very stout, she grew very rheumatic. Nothing would induce her to blame the kitchen. If you look at it today you may wonder – how any human being can have lived there. It was a basement house... The kitchen must have been almost always dark. In winter a little fan of gas was always burning. In summer a curtain of creeper made the room like a green cave... But nothing would induce her to leave it. Its been my home for forty years Miss she said...When all the children were married and the Master was dead, she had to choose – which of the children was to have her? 'I ought to be able to cut myself up among the lot of you' she said, putting her hands to her sides. But finally she decided for herself; as she always did… It must be Miss Ursula because she said, not in Miss Ursula's hearing – she's such a harum scarum thing – she wouldn't know if they sold her. 'She don't know what she has on her plate…'

What was to happen when she grew past work? Many family conclaves were held. But once more she settled that question for herself. She made no bones about it. She was perfectly prepared. She announced the news herself. She had taken a small room in a back street. She was quite decided. 'I'm going to have a bit of a holiday now' she said. She had saved up for that holiday. She was going to see the sights of London. She had never been to the tower; she had never been to Hampton Court…

Her room is hung with photographs. Her mind is like a family album. You turn up Uncle George; you turn up Aunt Emily… She remembers everything… She has a store of old anecdotes. It is surprising how much she noticed. Her room is crowded too with things people didnt want – 'things you threw away Miss.' A glass pig is one of them; also an Indian temple in silver – a present to Mrs Savery from a gentleman in India… She goes back far into the past, with her stories of the black days, of the rick burners, of the men with whips. And then there is the present moment… ticking away there on the mantlepiece among the family photographs is the clock. 'This clock' – every time you go to see her she reads out the inscription – 'This clock was given to Bridget Brien on her seventy fifth birthday in token of gratitude and affection,' here follows a string of names. 'Yes,' she said the other day, 'Its fifty five years now since I saw you all tumbling round your mother as she came down the stairs… And I'd live em all over again, every one of them.' Then, hitching a basket off a hook, she says, 'Now I'm off in my carriage and pair to my private park.' That is her way of alluding to the omnibus, and the private park is Kensington Gardens where she feeds the ducks and gossips with the nursemaids who are bringing up the next generation of Saverys.

One of Our Great Men (1930s?)

Outline for sketch

That is what his head master said of him – 'he'll be one of our great men.' And the head was not a man given to exaggeration, he had a vast experience of all kinds of boys…

The boy was rather like a sparrow to look at, small, frail, angular, insignificant, until he fixed his great dark eyes on you – a sparrow with the eyes of a hawk. His name was Rankin; and his initials F.A.R. gave him the nickname – Fairy – which stuck to him all through his life… The school was proud to own a Fairy. Nobody bullied him – he was scarcely even teased, as he flitted through those ancient cloisters, sometimes stopping, lost in thought, to read an inscription on a stone…

He won all the prizes and went to Cambridge with a scholarship. Stories began to be told about him there too… He read Greek as other people read the newspaper… He lived on black coffee and caviare… You always saw his light burning if you came back late. That grew into the legend that he practised black magic… Certainly it was true that he seemed asleep by day. In company he sat perfectly silent, like an idol, with his hands and feet drawn together.

'Ah, but you should hear him talk…' his friends said. About five in the morning he tapped on the window & came in. Other people said he never spoke at all. 'He's an illusion' they said, 'he doesnt exist…' They said they could see through him. So there were two parties – the believers and the scoffers.

Nobody knew where he spent his holidays. When term ended, he vanished. Only, from a postmark on a letter, it seemed that he sometimes visited D. an obscure little town in the midlands. One of his friends happened to find himself stranded there. He looked up Rankin in the directory. He rang the bell of a very dreary shabby little house – The Mimosas – on the outskirts.

'I had my excuse ready' he said, 'For I couldnt believe the Fairy lived there...'

He found him, reading aloud to an old lady in a bath chair. His mother kept a home for imbeciles... That was how he spent his holidays.

He went into a Bank when he left college – a very humble position for a man like that. But then, if you have an old mother in the midlands. And it was said that he forgot all about his examination... he was asleep...

His friends continued to believe in him. He was going to be one of the great men of his time. Probably he was working at a poem, after office hours, when he came back to that dreary London lodging in a back street. 'When is it coming out?' they pressed him. 'Anyhow, show us what you've written.' Or was it a history? Or was it a philosophy?... He was studying counter-point. Also he was teaching himself to paint. He was studying Chinese – and mathematics. Nothing was actually published. But 'Wait a little' his friends said. They waited.

The legend grew. That by itself was a proof of his greatness. It was fed with such strange odds and ends. For instance 'D'you see that chap?' said a man. He pointed to the Fairy in a tea shop, reading a newspaper, propped up on the cruet. He knows more about horses than any man outside a racing stable. He never went to a race meeting; but he knew the form of every horse in England. He was famous for his tips. You would hear of him from the most unlikely people and always something new. There is a gentleman who parades the front of a certain seaside town. He is known locally as 'The Puzzle King'... 'F.A.R. Rankin?' he said. 'He wins more prizes for the correct solution of cross word puzzles than any man in England – in Europe, I dare say' he added after a moment's pause. And Mr Peskett who kept the greengrocers shop at the corner of the street, thought him an infallible judge of rabbits...

You had to draw things from him, like a thread of wool from a tangled skein. There was a tortoise sunning itself on the little patch of green outside his window. 'D'you like tortoises, Fairy?' 'No'. His beautiful poet's eye regarded the tortoise. For ten minutes he was silent. His silences had something august about them as if he were watching Time from some peak of Eternity. And then he wd say, if somebody asked, 'D'you see that tortoise? The policeman gave it me.' Then the story of the policeman and the tortoise would be untangled. Time seemed to have no meaning for him. Other people married. He was very fond of children. But in love? Was he too poor to marry?... There was his old mother in the midlands – very old – very poor. Somebody once found him looking at the window opposite. He was watching the shadow of a woman doing her hair. 'Her gestures are so beautiful' he said. But he never approached any lady, beyond sending a valentine now and then...

And the young... began to ask questions. How had he got his reputation.

Still, his old friends, the faithful, always believed – he was going to be a great man. Wait till he retired, on his pension – then at last the day came – he got his pension. It was celebrated by a little banquet. Everybody spoke, not (as usually happens) about his triumphs, what he had done. But about what he was to do, now that he was free – now that he could give up business and devote himself to – the great book; the poem; the philosophy; or was it to be a history of China? Every sort of thing still seemed possible. He only nodded. And then he went off, free, at the age of sixty to show to the world that he was a great man. Between six and seven you can see him taking his daily walk, down through Temple Gardens, out on to the Embankment. He still walks just as he walked when he was a boy. That is to say he flits along and then he stops, sunk in thought, on the Bridge to look at the sun – to look at the Houses of Parliament. Many people see nothing in him – see that he has no existence. But to others, he is still, just as his head master said he would be – one of our great men. It depends of course upon what you mean by greatness – a very difficult question: different people hold different views.

11. Sophie Farrell.
Gift of Frederick R. Koch,
The Harvard Theatre Collection,
Houghton Library.

12. Saxon Sydney-Turner, Clive Bell, Julian Bell and Virginia Stephen on the beach at Studland Bay, Dorset.

JMK (1934)

Politics. Art. Dancing. Letters. Economics. Youth. The Future. Glands. Genealogies. Atlantis. Morality. Religion. Cambridge. Eton. The Drama. Society. Truth. Pigs. Sussex. The History of England. America. Optimism. Stammer. Old Books. Hume.

The pig was born in Berkshire, and no doubt cost its mother a pang or two as prize pigs do. But can it be proved that the prize pig was born on the hundred of the thane from whom the College in whose Chapel the organ is even now, at Evensong, pealing stole a thicket and therefore built a town six hundred years ago? (The art of biography is in its infancy. It has not yet learnt to walk without leading strings.) To cut the matter short, the prize pig was the father of a fine litter, not in Berkshire though, nor yet in the famous town where the Chapel is one of the sights of the civilised world, so that often on a fine summer evening a little knot of tourists will hang about the door asking each other who's that who's that? as the dignitaries go in and out.

Now it is a fact that Cyrus K. Pyecroft shot a little wad of chewing gum onto the turf the other evening accompanying the Professor. Famous in New York, famous on Wall Street, famous in Chicago, famous in Boston. By gum! he said.

Yes, a very famous man, he must be, who, in the summer pausing to sketch in the dry dust with the point of his shoe the plan – but the plan of what? When he had passed on, his head thrust forward, deep in talk, the tourists tried in vain to unriddle the criss-cross in the dust. A plan of some said one thing some another. It was none of these things though.

What was it then?

On June the 15th as the summer sun sunk over London the lights went up in Covent Garden. The Queen of England threw a rose to the ballet dancers, but the gentleman in full evening dress by her side, noted on the back of his shirt cuff that she was three quarters of an inch off the square. He was demonstrating to the most venerable of all masters – the Archbishop of the old established Russian Church of Dancing – this heresy – the fraction from the plan – when sure enough, as always happened that year between one and two in the morning – Downing Street unable to sleep, crept restlessly to the telephone, despairingly raised the receiver, and from the cavernous gloom of the deserted Cabinet Room, with Pitt ironically regarding the map that seemed on the point of being for ever rolled up, summoned the only trusty Counsellor, the one man on whom the fate of the Empire...

The sausage was still hot between his lips. Rose leaves and the torn muslin of ballet dancer's skirts were on the ground. He made him a tent of tulle; and there couchant, dictated. All the papers had it in large letters – next morning.

'But are you positive that the Capital A on the verso of the 10th folio is upside down?' he insisted, then sank back on his pillows.

England was off the gold standard; and he had at last, after years of research, recovered the only extant copy of the excessively rare pamphlet only three of which were in existence, one in the Kremlin, one at Pasadena – and now the third – the only known copy of that very obscure pamphlet for which he had been hunting, turning catalogues, browsing in dark booksellers' shops these twenty years.

So while they were calling the terrific news down the streets he lay, gazing at the narrow space between the great volumes – Hume, Locke, Berkeley, Malthus which swelled one after another in polished, in noble array underneath five apples by Cézanne. And then – his glance shot rapidly – there was Lady —— 's invitation to dinner, a little further along the shelf; and the statisticians were meeting – the philosophers and the anti-quaries and the genealogists, and the explorers. There was the expedition to that spot, now all running white capped waves, underneath slept the ruins of Atlantis. An old civilisation, a better civilisation? Atlantis. Had the bells there rung to higher services than those ringing now, outside? He heard them crying the news in the street. And shrugging his shoulders applied himself to the great green board on which were pinned sheets of symbols: a frolic of xs controlled by ys and embraced by more cryptic symbols still: which, if juggled together would eventually, he was sure, positive, produce the one word, the simple, the sufficient, the comprehensive word which will solve all problems forever. It was time to begin. He began.

13. John Maynard Keynes.

VI

Identifications, Editorial Notes, Acknowledgements and Works consulted

Identifications

Apostles: secret Cambridge undergraduate discussion club known as The Cambridge Conversazione Society or simply The Society; annual dinners for current and older members were held in London

Asheham: Woolfs' country home near Lewes, Sussex, 1912–19

Auden, W.H., 1907–73: poet, man of letters; published poems in *New Signatures* collection along with Lehmann, Spender and Julian Bell (Hogarth Press, 1932)

Audoux, Marguerite, 1863–1937: French novelist, author of *Marie-Claire*, the subtly naive story of an orphaned country girl

Beddoes, Thomas Lovell, 1803–49: poet, author of *Death's Jest-Book*

Bell, Angelica, see Garnett, Angelica

Bell, Clive, 1881–1964: art and literary critic, husband of Vanessa Bell, father of Julian and Quentin, member of the Bloomsbury Group

Bell, Colonel Cory: brother of Clive Bell

Bell, Julian, 1908–37: poet, son of Vanessa and Clive Bell, Apostle

Bell, Quentin, 1910–96: artist, art historian, biographer of Virginia Woolf, son of Vanessa and Clive Bell, brother of Julian Bell, member of the Bloomsbury Group

Bell, Vanessa, 1879–1961: painter, sister of Virginia Woolf, wife of Clive Bell, companion of Duncan Grant, mother of Julian, Quentin and Angelica, member of the Bloomsbury Group

Blackstick: Fairy in Thackeray's *The Rose and the Ring*, who interested herself in 'old books, young people, schools of practical instruction, rings, roses, sentimental affairs, etc.'

Blanco-White, Amber Reeves, 1887–1981: writer, lover of
H.G. Wells, later wife of the Fabian Rivers Blanco-White;
her two daughters attended Vanessa Bell's Charleston
school in 1917

Blunden, Edmund, 1896–1974: poet, critic

Blunt, Anthony, 1909–95: art historian, spy, Apostle

Bouvet, Mlle: former nun, French teacher of Julian Bell at
St Tropez

Braithwaite, Richard, 1900–90: philosopher, King's College
don, Apostle

Brereton, Mrs: friend of Roger Fry, governess (with her
daughter) at Charleston 1918–19

Buszards: tea rooms on Oxford Street, London

Camargo Society for the production of ballet founded in 1930

Cameron, Julia Margaret, 1815–79: photographer, great
aunt of Virginia Woolf, married to the jurist Charles Hay
Cameron (1795–1880)

Carpenter, Edward, 1844–1929: writer, sexual reformer, friend
of Roger Fry and E.M. Forster

Case, Janet, 1863–1937: classics teacher, feminist, journalist,
friend of Virginia Woolf

Cassis-sur-mer: village near Marseilles where Vanessa Bell,
Duncan Grant and others stayed from 1927 onwards

Cecil, Lord David, 1902–86: critic, biographer, Oxford English
professor, married to Rachel MacCarthy 1932

Charleston: country home near Firle, East Sussex, of Vanessa
Bell, Duncan Grant, Clive Bell and their children, from
1916; decorated by Vanessa, Duncan, Quentin and Angelica

Chatto & Windus: publishers of, among others, Lytton
Strachey, Roger Fry and Julian Bell's first volume of poems

Chen, Su Hua Ling, also known as Ling, Shu-hua, 1900–90:
Chinese writer, lover of Julian Bell, married to historian and
critic Chen Yuan (Julian Bell's Dean at Wuhan University)

Cole, **Horace de Vere**, 1881–1936: prankster, instigator of the *Dreadnought* Hoax

Cooper, **Lady Diana**, 1892–1986: actress, hostess, autobiographer, pupil of Janet Case

Dalton, **Hugh**, 1887–1962: Member of Parliament, opposition spokesman for foreign affairs, chairman of the Labour Party, 1936–7

Davies, **Margaret Llewelyn**, 1861–1944: general secretary of the Women's Co-operative Guild (1889–1922), campaigner for women's causes, good friend of Leonard and Virginia Woolf

Dreadnought: biggest and most powerful British battleship of the time, secretly built in 1906, flagship of the Home Fleet in 1910. *Dreadnought* became a general name for a class of battleship superior to all predecessors

Duckworth family: Julia Prinsep Stephen's first husband was Herbert Duckworth (1833–70); they had three children, George (1868–1934), Stella (1869–97) and Gerald (1870–1937)

Edwards, Eva: governess at Charleston, 1917

Farrell, Sophia, 1861–1942: Stephen family cook

Firle: Sussex village near Charleston; Firle Beacon is the highest point on the Sussex downs

Fisher, **Admiral Sir William Wordsworth**, 1875–1937, cousin of Virginia Woolf, served as Flag Commander of the *Dreadnought* during the hoax

Forster, **Edward Morgan**, 1879–1970: novelist, essayist, critic, biographer, Apostle, member of the Bloomsbury Group. His biography of King's College don Goldsworthy Lowes Dickinson (1934) led to Julian Bell's essay-letter to Forster on war and peace

Freshwater: village at the western end of the Isle of Wight, where Julia Margaret Cameron and Alfred Lord Tennyson lived with their families, as did Anne Thackeray Ritchie; later Virginia Woolf took the name and setting for her comedy of Victorian life (1923/1935)

Fry, Roger, 1866–1934: art critic, painter, Apostle, member of the Bloomsbury Group, lover of Vanessa Bell, 1911–13; subject of an essay-letter by Julian Bell; biography by Virginia Woolf (1940)

Garnett, Angelica, b. 1918: artist, writer, daughter of Vanessa Bell and Duncan Grant, married David Garnett in 1942

Garnett, David, known as Bunny, 1892–1981: writer, editor, member of the Bloomsbury Group, married Angelica Bell in 1942

Garsington: Oxfordshire manor house, country home of Lady Ottoline Morrell, 1915–28

Gordon Square: Bloomsbury square where the Stephens, Stracheys, Bells, Woolfs and Keyneses all lived at various times and addresses

Grant, Duncan, 1885–1978: painter, cousin of Lytton Strachey, companion of Vanessa Bell, father of Angelica Garnett and member of the Bloomsbury Group

Graves, Sally, b. 1914: niece of Robert Graves

Hardy, Thomas, 1840–1928: novelist and poet; in his poem 'Shreckhorn' he compared the alp to Leslie Stephen

Harris, Lilian, d. 1950: assistant secretary, Women's Co-operative Guild, lifelong friend of Margaret Llewelyn Davies

Higgens, Grace: cook at Charleston for fifty-two years

Hogarth Press: founded by the Woolfs in 1917 originally to print stories and poems rejected by commercial publishers

Holman, Portia, 1903–83: doctor, later psychiatrist, friend of Julian Bell, worked with Spanish Medical Aid in Madrid during the Spanish Civil War

Hope, Lottie: servant of the Bells in Gordon Square

Hopwood, Admiral R.A., 1868–1949: naval officer and poet, known for the Kiplingesque 'Laws of the Navy'

Huxley, T.H., 1825–95: scientist, author, agnostic, Darwinian

Hyndman, Tony, 1911–80: lover of Stephen Spender, deserted from the International Brigade in Spain

International Brigade: Communist-backed brigade of volunteers from various countries formed in 1936 to fight for the government cause in Spain

J.: unidentified in Vanessa Bell's memoir of Julian; perhaps Jane Simone Bussy, 1906–60: painter, daughter of Dorothy and Simon Bussy, friend of Julian Bell in the 1920s

Jebb, Sir Richard Claverhouse, 1841–1905: Cambridge Greek scholar and Apostle whose letters describing Anne Thackeray Ritchie's writing were published in 1907

Keynes, John Maynard, 1883–1946: economist, King's College don, Apostle, member of the Bloomsbury Group

Kidd, Harriet A., d. 1917: clerk in the Women's Co-operative Guild office from 1906

Lamb, Walter, 1882–1968: classicist, later secretary of the Royal Academy, brother of the painter Henry Lamb

Lawrence, John Laird Mair, 1st Baron, 1811–79: Viceroy of India, 1863–9

Left Book Club: publishing venture of Victor Gollancz with John Strachey and Harold Laski to oppose the rise of Fascism by circulating political books

Lehmann, John, 1907–87: poet, man of letters, editor, assistant in the Hogarth Press in 1931–3, partner 1938–46; published *A Garden Revisited* (1931) with the Hogarth Press and poems in Hogarth's *New Signatures* collection (1932) along with Auden, Spender and Julian Bell

Leighton House: Victorian London museum and art gallery with an exotic Eastern interior

Leighton Park School: Quaker public school Julian Bell attended, 1922–6

Lewes, George Henry, 1817–78: writer, partner of George Eliot

Lopokova, Lydia, 1891–1981: ballerina, married to J.M. Keynes

Lowell, James Russell, 1819–91: poet, essayist, diplomat, friend of Leslie Stephen, godfather to Virginia Woolf

Lucas, Frank Laurence (Peter), 1894–1967: writer, classicist, King's College English don, tutor of Julian Bell, Apostle

Luce, Gordon Hannington, 1889–1979: poet, teacher, Apostle

Lytton, Edward Robert Bulwer, 1831–91: Viceroy of India, friend of Jane Maria Strachey who named her son after him

MacCarthy, Sir Desmond, 1877–1952: literary and dramatic critic, Apostle, member of the Bloomsbury Group, married to Molly MacCarthy, father of Michael, Rachel and Dermod MacCarthy who attended Vanessa Bell's Charleston school; involved with Fry in the post-Impressionist exhibition of 1910; gave the Leslie Stephen Lecture at Cambridge on Leslie Stephen in 1937

Mad Mary: Mary Elizabeth Wilson, servant engaged by Vanessa Bell in 1920, whose madness was the subject of a Memoir Club paper by Vanessa Bell

Maitland, Frederic William, 1850–1906: legal historian, Apostle, biographer of Leslie Stephen

Martin, Kingsley, 1897–1969: editor of the *New Statesman and Nation*

May, Admiral Sir William Henry: Commander of the Home Fleet, 1909–11

McKenna, Reginald, 1863–1943: 1st Lord of the Admiralty, 1908–11

Memoir Club, The: started by Molly MacCarthy after the First World War to bring the Bloomsbury Group back together by writing short memoirs for the amusement of one another; lasted until Clive Bell's death in 1964

Meredith, George, 1828–1909: novelist and poet. His 'Love in the Valley' was a favourite of Leslie Stephen's; in his novel *The Egoist* Meredith took Stephen as a model for the austere Vernon Whitford, whom he described as 'Phoebus Apollo turned fasting friar'

Moore, George Edward, 1873–1958: Cambridge philosopher, Apostle, author of *Principia Ethica* (1903) from which Bloomsbury took some of its basic values

Morrell, Lady Ottoline Cavendish-Bentinck, 1873–1938: half-sister to the Duke of Portland, hostess, patron of the arts, married to Philip Morrell

Outram, Sir James, 1803–63: Indian army general, hero of the Mutiny

Owen's School: Dame Alice Owen's School that Julian Bell attended 1919–21

Pater, Clara, 1841–1910: Oxford classics tutor, sister of Walter Pater, teacher of Virginia Woolf

Pattle family: included the Bengal civil servant James (1775–1845), his wife Adeline d'Étang (1793–1845) and their seven celebrated daughters (known as 'Pattledom') who included Julia Margaret Cameron, Sarah Prinsep and Virginia Woolf's grandmother Maria Jackson

Pinault, Henri: French teacher in Paris with whose family Julian Bell stayed during his year in Paris

Playfair, Edward, b. 1909: close friend and contemporary of Julian Bell at King's College; Treasury official

Prinsep family: included Sarah Pattle Prinsep (1816–87), her husband the Indian civil servant Henry Thoby Prinsep (1792–1878) and their painter son Val Prinsep (1838–1904), disciple of G.F. Watts, whose patrons the Prinseps were in their Little Holland House circle in London and at Freshwater

Ramsey, Frank, 1903–30: philosopher, King's College don, Apostle, husband of Lettice Ramsey

Ramsey, Lettice, 1898–1985: photographer, wife of Frank Ramsey; as a widow, lover of Julian Bell

Read, Elizabeth: social worker, admirer of Virginia Woolf, companion of Gilbert Denny

Regent Square: Georgian Square, London, WC1, where Vanessa Bell had a studio in 1919

Rhondda, Viscountess Margaret Haig Thomas, 1883–1958: feminist, founder-editor of *Time and Tide*

Ritchie, Anne Isabella Thackeray, 1837–1919: novelist and memoirist, eldest daughter of William Makepeace Thackeray, whose younger daughter Minnie was Leslie Stephen's first wife; married her cousin Richmond Thackeray Ritchie (1854–1912), becoming Lady Ritchie when he was made a Civil Service knight in 1907

Roberts, Frederick Sleigh, 1st Earl, 1832–1914: field marshal

Rodmell: Sussex village near Lewes, location of the Woolfs' Monk's House

St Tropez, France: location of a villa the Bells stayed at in 1921–2

Salvini, Tommaso, 1829–1915: Italian actor

Scott James, R.A., 1878–1959: editor of *The London Mercury*

Seend: Wiltshire village, location of Cleeve House, home of Clive Bell's family

Selwood, Mabel: Julian and Quentin Bell's nurse and governess

Smyth, Dame Ethel, 1858–1944: composer, feminist and autobiographer, friend of Virginia Woolf

Society, The: see Apostles

Soutar, Helen, 1909–85: Girton undergraduate, 1928–31; lover of Julian Bell

Spanish Medical Aid: English committee formed to provide medical services for government forces in the Spanish Civil War; Julian Bell was one of its ambulance drivers

Spender, Stephen, 1909–95: poet, man of letters; visited Spain, 1936–7; published poems in *New Signatures* collection along with Auden, Lehmann and Julian Bell (1932)

Stansfeld, Sir James, 1820–98: politician, Radical MP, uncle of Janet Case

Stephen, Adrian, 1893–1948: psychiatrist, brother of Vanessa Bell, Thoby Stephen and Virginia Woolf

Stephen, Ann, b. 1916: daughter of Adrian Stephen, undergraduate at Newnham

Stephen, Caroline Emelia, 1834–1909: sister of Leslie and Fitzjames Stephen, Quaker author and philanthropist

Stephen, Sir James, 1789–1859: father of Leslie, Caroline and Fitzjames Stephen, colonial under-secretary, slavery abolitionist, historian

Stephen, Sir James Fitzjames, 1829–94: brother of Leslie and Caroline Stephen, essayist, judge, Apostle

Stephen, Jane Catherine Venn, 1793–1875: mother of Leslie, Caroline and Fitzjames Stephen

Stephen, Julia Prinsep, 1846–95: 'celebrated beauty and philanthropist' (*ODNB*), married to Herbert Duckworth, 1867–70; their children were George, Stella, and Gerald. Married Leslie Stephen, 1878–95, mother of Vanessa Bell, Thoby Stephen, Virginia Woolf and Adrian Stephen

Stephen, Sir Leslie, 1832–1904: biographer, critic, historian of ideas, mountaineer, editor, brother of Caroline and Fitzjames Stephen; married Harriet (Minny) Thackeray (1840–75): their child was Laura Makepeace Stephen (1870–1945). Married Julia Prinsep Stephen in 1878; their children were Vanessa Bell, Thoby Stephen, Virginia Woolf and Adrian Stephen. The Leslie Stephen lectureship was established in his honour at Cambridge and given in 1937 by Desmond MacCarthy on Leslie Stephen

Stephen, (Julian) Thoby, 1880–1906: son of Leslie and Julia Stephen, brother of Vanessa Bell, Virginia Woolf and Adrian Stephen

Strachey Family: included Jane Maria Grant, Lady Strachey (1840–1928), her husband General Sir Richard Strachey (1817–1908) and their ten children – among whom were Dorothy Bussy, Philippa, Pernel, Lytton, James. Duncan Grant was Lady Strachey's nephew

Studland, Dorset: coastal holiday place for Bloomsbury, 1909–10

Sydney-Turner, Saxon, 1880–1962: Treasury official, Apostle, member of the Bloomsbury Group

Tavistock Square: Bloomsbury square where the Woolfs lived, 1924–39

Taylor, Sir Henry, 1800–86: author, friend of Julia Margaret Cameron

Terry, Dame Ellen, 1847–1928: actress, married to G.F. Watts, 1864–5

Troubridge, Laura Gurney, Lady, 1858–1929: granddaughter of Virginia Woolf's great aunt Sarah Prinsep (see Pattle family); author of *Memories of Reflections* (1925)

Vaughan, Dame Janet, 1899–1993: haematologist and radiobiologist, cousin of the Stephens, socialist, worked with Spanish Medical Aid committee during the Civil War

Verrall, A.W., 1851–1912: Cambridge classical scholar, editor, translator, critic, Apostle

Watts, George Frederic, 1817–1904: painter, whose patrons were the Prinseps; married, 1864–5, to Ellen Terry; divorced, then married Mary Tyler in 1886, who wrote his biography

Wissett Lodge: Suffolk farmhouse where Duncan Grant, David Garnett, Vanessa Bell and her children lived in 1916

Women's Co-operative Guild: founded in 1883 as an auxiliary of the Consumer Co-operative Movement; became the largest association of English working class women. Its policies were progressive and feminist. Margaret Llewelyn Davies was its general secretary for thirty-three years

Women's Institutes: self-governing groups of women engaging in educational, dramatic, social and political activities, started in Britain in 1915. Virginia Woolf was involved with the Rodmell Women's Institute

Woolf, Leonard, 1880–1969: married Virginia Stephen, 1912; imperial civil servant, writer, editor, critic, political theorist, Labour Party advisor, publisher, Apostle, member of the Bloomsbury Group

Editorial Notes

Information on Virginia Woolf's published essays is from B.J. Kirkpatrick and Stuart N. Clarke's *A Bibliography of Virginia Woolf*, 4th edition, 1997. First reprintings only of Woolf's essays are noted below. References to Woolf's *Collected Essays* are to Leonard Woolf's four-volume edition (1966–7); references to her *Essays* are to Andrew McNeillie's incomplete four-volume edition (1986–94).

Julian Bell

The memoirs of Julian Bell by Virginia Woolf and Vanessa Bell were first published in a somewhat different form in *Cahiers victoriens et édouardiens*, 62 (October 2005), 167–203. Virginia Woolf's untitled memoir of Julian Bell has been preserved in Special Collections of the University of Sussex in a twenty-two-page holograph manuscript (Monks House Papers A.8). Her earlier unpublished dramatic sketch of Julian (given the title 'JB', but perhaps not by her) is a typescript revision of pages from a notebook, both of which are at Sussex (A.18, B.2.e). The sketch may have been intended for the *Charleston Bulletin*, which once advertised a contribution to be entitled 'The Life and Adventures of J. Bell by Virginia Woolf'. Vanessa Bell's pencilled notebook is in the twentieth-century archives of King's College, Cambridge (Charleston Papers Cha/3/1/3). The holograph manuscripts have only a few insertions and minor cancellations. Julian Bell's letter to Virginia Woolf is also in the twentieth-century archives of King's College. Virginia Woolf's letters to Julian Bell were edited by Joanne Trautmann Banks in *Modern Fiction Studies*, 30 (Summer, 1984), 188, 196–7.

In editing the two memoirs, I have omitted the cancellations and incorporated the insertions. Possessive apostrophes have been added and an occasional bracketed word when required for clarity. Contractions have been left mostly as they are, sometimes with periods, sometimes not. Ampersands have also been retained to distinguish them from *and*s. Virginia Woolf's uses of single and double quotation marks have been kept but made consistent. A few slight errors such as a word repeated at the start of a page, the use of a period instead of a comma, or a missing parenthesis or quotation mark have been silently corrected. Some spacing between lines or pages in Woolf's memoir has also been regularised and paragraph indentations made consistent, but I have attempted to retain something of the spacing and paragraphing in Vanessa's notebook. Family initials have been expanded the first time they are given; the full names of others have been supplied in brackets when they are first mentioned. In editing the type-written sketch I have also added speakers' names in some places. I am very grateful to Peter Stansky for information about Julian Bell.

Leslie Stephen

'A Daughter's Impressions' is taken from the opening of the last chapter, entitled 'The Sunset (1902–1904)', of Frederic William Maitland's *The Life and Letters of Leslie Stephen* published by Stephen's stepson's firm Duckworth & Co. in November, 1906, and reprinted in *Essays*, vol. 1.

'A Daughter's Memories' appeared in *The Times*, 28th November 1932, with the following editorial note: *'Sir Leslie Stephen, philosopher, man of letters, editor of the Dictionary of National Biography and mountaineer, was born on November 28, 1832.'* The memoir was originally reprinted but without the *Times* subheadings in *The Captain's Death Bed and Other Essays* edited by Leonard Woolf in 1950. The heading of the *Times* article has been rearranged here.

Caroline Emelia Stephen

'Obituary'. The anonymous obituary was published in the Church of England paper the *Guardian*, 21st April 1909 and reprinted in the American Quaker paper the *Friend* in August. Reprinted in *Essays*, vol. 1.

Anne Thackeray Ritchie

'*Blackstick Papers*: Essays' is an anonymous review of *Blackstick Papers*, so titled, in the *Times Literary Supplement*, 19th November 1908, the year the book was published. Reprinted in *Essays*, vol. 1.

'Tribute: Lady Ritchie' is an anonymous essay entitled 'Lady Ritchie' in the *Times Literary Supplement* 6th March 1919. Reprinted in *Essays*, vol. 3.

'Obituary by Leonard Woolf' is unsigned in *The Times*, 28th February 1919. Reprinted in *Essays*, vol. 3.

'The Enchanted Organ: Letters' is a signed review entitled 'The Enchanted Organ' in *The Nation and Athenaeum*, 15th March 1924, of *Letters of Anne Thackeray Ritchie*, ed. Hester Ritchie (1924). Reprinted in *The Moment*, edited by Leonard Woolf, 1947.

Julian Margaret Cameron

'Introduction' is to *Victorian Photographs of Famous Men & Fair Women* published by the Hogarth Press in 1926 with another introduction on the photographs by Roger Fry. Woolf's essay was reprinted in *A Bloomsbury Group Reader* in 1993.

'Biography by Julia Prinsep Stephen' was published in the *Dictionary of National Biography* in 1886.

Jane Maria Strachey

'Lady Strachey' is from *The Nation and Athenaeum*, 22nd

December 1928, signed 'V.W.'. Reprinted in *Books and Portraits*, ed. Mary Lyon (1977).

'J.M.S.: Notes'. The last five notes headed 'From *Virginia Woolf*' in a collection of typed reminiscences entitled J.M.S., 1840–1929 [sic], Monks House Papers, Ad 25, University of Sussex Library. Unpublished.

Roger Fry

'A Series of Impressions', written sometime after Vanessa Bell's memoir of Fry (published in her *Sketches in Pen and Ink*) which is dated October, 1934, following Fry's death in September. Woolf's impressions were first edited by Jocelyn Bartkevicius, *Iowa Review*, 22 (Winter 1992), 129–31, and then by Diane Gillespie as a Bloomsbury Heritage Pamphlet (London, 1994). Gillespie's edition includes all the insertions and cancellations in Virginia Woolf's typescript with holograph changes (which is now in the Berg Public Library). I have used Gillespie's edition, adding an occasional word or punctuation for clarity and incorporating Woolf's insertions without indicating them as such; I have also omitted cancellations, partial repetitions of phrases, indications of doubtful readings and editorial comment. I am grateful to Gillespie for her help with this transcription.

'Memorial Exhibition Address' was delivered at the opening of the Roger Fry Memorial Exhibition at the Bristol Museum and Art Gallery, 12th July 1935, and privately printed as *The Roger Fry Memorial Exhibition: An Address* the same year. It was first reprinted as 'Roger Fry' in *The Moment and Other Essays*, ed. Leonard Woolf (1947).

Janet Case

'An Old Pupil's Recollections' is an unsigned letter to *The Times*, 22nd July 1937, p. 16. Never reprinted.

'Miss Case' is a sketch from a 1903 diary published in *A Passionate Apprentice: The Early Journals of Virginia Woolf*, ed. Mitchell A. Leaska (1990), pp. 181–4. Woolf's manuscript deletions have been omitted here.

Lady Ottoline Morrell

'Obituary Letter' appeared in two early editions of *The Times*, 28th April 1938, but was omitted from later ones by a mistake, according to the paper as reported by Woolf in her diary (29th April 1938); reprinted in an appendix to volume 5 of the diary. A fragmentary typescript of the letter with corrections by Leonard Woolf is in the Berg Collection of the New York Public Library. The 1909 diary has been published in a collection of sketches called *Carlyle's House and Other Sketches* by the editor David Bradshaw. The epitaph by T.S. Eliot and Virginia Woolf is from an unpublished letter of hers, 7th July 1939, as cited in Seymour's biography of Ottoline Morrell.

Memories of a Working Women's Guild

'Life as We Have Known It'. Originally published in the *Yale Review* (September 1930) with names disguised, then revised with actual names and significant alterations and additions as 'Introductory Letter to Margaret Llewelyn Davies' in *Life as We Have Known It* by Co-operative Working Women, edited by Davies, Hogarth Press, 1931. Leonard Woolf reprinted the first version in *The Captain's Death Bed* (1950) with the following footnote: 'These pages, written in 1930, relating to the Women's Co-operative Guild, are addressed to a former officer of this organisation who had placed in Mrs. Woolf's hands a collection of letters written by its members.' A more detailed footnote was given in the *Yale Review*. The revised version of Woolf's essay has never been reprinted separately from *Life as We Have Known It*, anthologists all having followed Leonard Woolf in reproducing the early version. For a discussion of the two versions, see Naomi Black, *Virginia Woolf as Feminist*.

The Dreadnought *Hoax*

'*Dreadnought* Notes' is a four-page typescript with holograph insertions, three of which (numbered 20, 21, 22 in the Monks House papers of the University of Sussex, A.27) were originally published as an appendix in Quentin Bell's *Virginia Woolf*, vol. 1. In the margins of this typescript Woolf noted in pencil the following series of topics for her talk: 'A. & D. go to McKenna', 'Rules made', 'W.W.'s visit on Sunday', 'W.F.'s rage', 'A. gives addresses', 'Officers call on D.', 'D.G. alone', 'Won't fight'. A fourth page, numbered 24 and called 'The Real Emperor' in the margin, is a one-page typescript in the Berg Collection, New York Public Library (Reel 12, M114, of the microfilm) which begins with the last words of a sentence about the officer's mess and then has the added note about the real Emperor of Abyssinia; most of this page was published in Hermione Lee's biography. In editing Woolf's notes from the original rough typescript I have altered the paragraphing slightly and corrected typing errors.

'Interview' appeared in the *Daily Mirror and* was reprinted by Stephen Barkway in the *Virginia Woolf Bulletin* (January 2006).

The Cook

'The Cook' is preserved in two undated, unpublished typescript drafts of four and eight pages in the Monks House Papers of the University of Sussex (A.13.d, e). Possibly begun in 1929, the sketch was meticulously transcribed and printed by Susan Dick in the *Woolf Studies Annual*, III (1997), 122–42. Dick based her version on Draft B, which I have followed. I have incorporated the insertions and some of the substantive deletions from Woolf's Draft B, as well as an occasional editorial emendation, all of which are given in Dick's transcription. Punctuation has also occasionally been regularised. I am much indebted to Dick's introduction for information on Sophia Farrell. Her note to Leonard Woolf is quoted in Victoria Glendinning's biography of him.

One of Our Great Men

'One of Our Great Men' is from an undated, unpublished typescript with holograph revisions headed 'Outline for sketch called One of our great men'. Preserved in the Monks House Papers of the University of Sussex (A.13.c). A cover sheet not in Virginia Woolf's hand identifies it as 'story about S.S.T'. I am grateful to Susan Dick, and Sarah M. Hall for help with deciphering the holograph revisions. In editing the typescript I have regularised capitalisation and some punctuation and corrected misspellings and mistypings. The ellipses in the text are Woolf's.

JMK

'JMK' is a three-page notebook sketch headed 'JMK' preserved in the Berg Collection of the New York Public Library, vol. 7, 73–7 of Woolf's manuscripts. Published in *The Charleston Magazine*, Spring/Summer, 1995, 5–6, and reprinted in *The Bloomsbury Group*, revised ed., 274–5. In transcribing the sketch I have regularised capitalisation and punctuation and omitted cancellations as well as a few words Woolf neglected to cancel. The handwriting is difficult and a few of the readings are conjectural.

Acknowledgements and Works consulted

I am indebted to the Estate of Virginia Woolf for permission to publish Woolf's texts, to the Estate of Vanessa Bell and Henrietta Garnett for permission to publish Vanessa Bell's memoir of Julian Bell, and to the estate of Leonard Woolf for permission to publish his obituary of Lady Ritchie. For permission to publish Julian Bell's letter to Virginia Woolf I am grateful to Anne Olivier Bell who for nearly forty years now has offered hospitality, friendship, support and scepticism.

The twentieth-century archives of King's College, Cambridge, the Special Collections of the University of Sussex Library, the library of Victoria College of the University of Toronto, and the New York Public Library's Berg Collection have kindly provided copies of memoirs and other manuscripts. E.H. Pridmore and Rosalind Moad of the King's College archives, and Peter Stansky, have all generously given valuable information and advice. Susan Dick has helped once again with deciphering Woolf's handwriting and typewriting. To Christine Reynier, editor of the Bloomsbury issue of *Cahiers victoriens et édouardiens*, I am indebted for first publishing Woolf and Bell's memoirs of Julian. Anne Olivier Bell's edition of Virginia Woolf's diaries and Andrew McNeillie's edition of her essays have been very helpful with identifications.

Jeremy Crow of the Society of Authors has been of great assistance throughout the collecting of the texts in *The Platform of Time*. What I owe at all stages of the editing and writing to the advice, encouragement, criticism, laughter and love of Naomi Black, I cannot express.

Works cited or consulted
Auden, W.H., *The English Auden*, ed. Edward Mendelson
(1977)

Barkway, Stephen, 'The *Dreadnought* Hoax: The Aftermath for "Prince Sanganya" and "His" Cousins', *Virginia Woolf Bulletin*, 21 (Jan. 2006)

Bell, Julian, *Essays, Poems and Letters*, ed. Quentin Bell (1936)

— ed., *We Did Not Fight: 1914–18 Experiences of War Resisters* (1935)

Bell, Quentin, *A Biography of Virginia Woolf*, 2 vols. (1972)

— *Elders and Betters* (1995)

Bell, Vanessa, *Letters*, ed. Regina Marler (1993)

— *Sketches in Pen and Ink*, ed. Lia Giachero (1997)

Black, Naomi, *Virginia Woolf as Feminist* (2004)

Caine, Barbara, *Bombay to Bloomsbury: A Biography of the Strachey Family* (2005)

Charleston Bulletin, 1923–27 (?), British Library manuscripts

DNB: *Dictionary of National Biography*, Compact Edition (1975)

Ford, Colin, *Julia Margaret Cameron: 19th Century Photographer of Genius* (2003)

Forster, E.M., 'Virginia Woolf', *Two Cheers for Democracy* (1951)

Garnett, Henrietta, *Anny: A Life of Isabella Thackeray Ritchie* (2004)

Glendinning, Victoria, *Leonard Woolf* (2006)

Humm, Maggie, ed., *Snapshots of Bloomsbury* (2006)

Keynes, J.M. *Collected Writings*, ed. Donald Moggridge, vol. XXVIII (1983)

Kirkpatrick, B.J., and Stuart N. Clarke, *A Bibliography of Virginia Woolf*, 4th ed. (1997)

Laurence, Patricia, *Lily Briscoe's Chinese Eyes: Bloomsbury, Modernism, and China* (2003)

Lee, Hermione, *Virginia Woolf* (1996)

Maitland, F.W., *The Life and Letters of Leslie Stephen* (1906)

Morrell, Ottoline, *Ottoline at Garsington: Memoirs of Lady Ottoline Morrell 1915–1918*, ed. Robert Gathorne-Hardy (1974)

ODNB: *Oxford Dictionary of National Biography* (2004)

Raby, Alister, *Virginia Woolf's Wise and Witty Quaker Aunt: A Biographical Sketch of Caroline Emelia Stephen* (2002)

Reid, Panthea, *Art and Affection: A Life of Virginia Woolf* (1996)

Richardson, Elizabeth P., *A Bloomsbury Iconography* (1989)

Rosenbaum, S.P., *Victorian Bloomsbury, Edwardian Bloomsbury, Georgian Bloomsbury: The Early Literary History of the Bloomsbury Group*, 3 vols. (1987–2003)

— ed., *The Bloomsbury Group: A Collection of Memoirs and Commentary*, rev. ed. (1995)

— ed., *A Bloomsbury Group Reader* (1993)

Seymour, Miranda, *Ottoline Morrell* (1998)

Spalding, Frances, *Duncan Grant* (1997)

— *Vanessa Bell* (1983)

Stansky, Peter, and William Abrahams, *Journey to the Frontier: Julian Bell and John Cornford* (1966)

Stephen, Adrian, *The Dreadnought Hoax*, introduction by Quentin Bell (1936/1983)

Thomas, Hugh, *The Spanish Civil War* (2003)

Virginia Woolf: Major Authors on CD-Rom, ed. Mark Hussey (1996)

Wikipedia, the Free Encyclopedia: http://en.wikipedia.org

Woolf, Leonard, *An Autobiography*, 2 vols. (1980)

— *Letters*, ed. Frederic Spotts (1989)

Woolf, Virginia, *Carlyle's House and Other Sketches,* ed. David Bradshaw (2003)

— *Collected Essays*, ed. Leonard Woolf, 4 vols. (1966–7)

— *Diaries*, ed. Anne Olivier Bell assisted by Andrew McNeillie, 5 vols., (1977–84)

— *Essays*, ed. Andrew McNeillie, 4 vols. (1986–94)

— *Freshwater: A Comedy*, ed. Lucio Ruotolo (1976)

— *Letters*, ed. Nigel Nicolson and Joanne Trautmann, 6 vols. (1975–80)

— *The Moment and Other Essays*, ed. Leonard Woolf (1947)

— *Moments of Being: Autobiographical Writings*, ed. Jeanne Schulkind and Hermione Lee, 3rd ed. (2002)

— *A Passionate Apprentice: The Early Journals of Virginia Woolf*, ed. Mitchell A. Leaska (1990)

— *Roger Fry*, ed. Diane F. Gillespie (1940/1995)

— 'A Society', *Complete Shorter Fiction*, ed. Susan Dick, 2nd ed. (1989), 124–36

— 'Some New Woolf Letters', ed. Joanne Trautmann Banks, *Modern Fiction Studies*, 30 (Summer, 1984), 175–202

— *Three Guineas*, ed. Naomi Black (1938/2001)

Woolmer, J. Howard, *A Checklist of the Hogarth Press* (1986)

Acknowledgements for photographs

p.44: 1. Tate, London 2006. 2. National Portrait Gallery, London.

p.98: 3. Harvard Theatre Collection. 4. and 5. National Portrait Gallery, London.

p.117: 6. National Portrait Gallery, London.

p.136: 7. Harvard Theatre Collection. 8. National Portrait Gallery, London.

p.170: 9. National Executive Committee of the Co-operative Women's Guild. 10. Mary Evans Picture Library.

p.188: 11. Harvard Theatre Collection. 12. Tate, London 2006.

p.191: 13. National Portrait Gallery, London.

Index

S.P. Rosenbaum is the author of a three-volume literary history of Old Bloomsbury: *Victorian Bloomsbury* (1987), *Edwardian Bloomsbury* (1994) and *Georgian Bloomsbury* (2003). His essays on Bloomsbury have been collected in *Aspects of Bloomsbury* (1998). He has also edited Virginia Woolf's *Women & Fiction: The Manuscript Versions of* A Room of One's Own (1992), *A Bloomsbury Group Reader* (1993), and *The Bloomsbury Group: A Collection of Memoirs and Criticism* (1975, revised edition, 1995). He is now writing a history of The Memoir Club.